TEACHING THE
VERY ABLE
CHILD

Belle Wallace

©Belle Wallace

First published 1983
by Ward Lock Educational Ltd
47 Marylebone Lane
London W1M 6AX

A Ling Kee Company

ISBN 0 7062 4228 9

British Library Cataloguing in Publication Data

Wallace, Belle
   Teaching the very able child.
   1. Gifted children – Education
   I. Title
   371.95   LC3993

   ISBN 0-7062-4228-9

262

Set in 10 on 11pt Lasercomp Plantin
by MS Filmsetting Ltd, Frome, Somerset
and printed in Hong Kong

Contents

Acknowledgments

This book is dedicated to the many teachers in Essex who have given me so much personal encouragement and support together with their professional dedication and expertise. Teachers have been prepared to do what can only be described as the 'tenth mile', and I regard myself as the privileged scribe who is recording the collaborative result of many people's work. Most in-service education courses have taken place after school; most curriculum extension courses have involved teachers voluntarily working at weekends and during holidays. Preparation for those courses has been done mainly in teachers' 'spare' time and is evidence of their professional commitment and genuine concern for children's educational, emotional and social needs.

We have worked as a team and I am indebted to so many who have discussed problems, helped to refine ideas, supplied additional information and generally contributed advice and suggestions. It is impossible to list all the teachers who have made valuable contributions and given their time, but the following people have taken leadership roles in group workshops, administration of courses or the preparation of curriculum extension projects:

Barry Adams
Stephen Baines
Joyce Benson
Barbara Bexley
Mike Dyer
Peggy Garrett
Robert Glanz
Terri Gregory
Jim Hind
Joan Hurdle
Glyn Jarrett
Chris Martin
John Llewellyn-Jones
Marilyn Lampey
Bill Langlois
Mary Lewis

John Morris
John Mulrenan
Diana Naylor
Thea Prisk
Gwen Porteous
John Sapwell
Pat Smith
Tony Smith
Dave Stamp
Davina Tweddle
Valerie Webb
Julian Whybra
Eleanor Williams
Elizabeth Woodfield
Ruth Yates

Particular appreciation must be expressed for the guidance and support of John Acklaw, County Psychologist, Essex, and to the team of educational psychologists who have supported the work incorporating extra tasks of assessment and guidance into an already heavy schedule.

In addition, Grace Collier-Bradley, Director of the Leonardo Trust, Frank Sherwood, Education Officer for the National Association of Gifted Children, and Dr Trevor Kerry, School of Education, Nottingham, gave valuable help and advice in refining and clarifying ideas.

Finally, a very special debt is owed to my husband for his patient understanding and constant support.

Introduction

This is an essentially practical book which looks at the education of very able children. It is concerned with the ordinary classroom and the problems and possible solutions to the day-to-day queries and uncertainties which many parents, pupils and teachers face.

The conclusions and recommendations are the result of a collaborative exploration and exchange of ideas which I have had with teachers and parents in Essex since September 1978, when I took up the newly-created post of County Advisory Teacher for Exceptionally Able Children. Between 1978 and 1982, as part of the current programme in Essex on work with very able children, approximately 4,000 teachers have attended in-service education courses; 790 primary children and 540 secondary children have attended extra-curricula day and residential courses; I have visited 300 primary schools and 65 secondary schools to discuss in depth the needs of individual exceptionally able pupils and to structure appropriate curriculum extension. (The background to this current programme is set out in Appendix A.)

The working brief of the Advisory Teacher encapsulated basic principles from which any county or area provision for very able pupils could develop.

There were two equally important tasks: to help teachers develop

1 awareness of the particular needs of very able pupils;
2 skills in identification techniques which could be used in a classroom.

Until teachers are made aware of a particular problem, they cannot begin to examine why it exists, nor think constructively about its solution. Consequently, it was essential to discuss very able children in the contexts of under-achievement and behaviour problems as well as in the context of providing additional resources for high-achieving children.

The residential curriculum extension courses for very able pupils which had taken place before 1978 had provided the teachers who had been involved with first-hand experience of working with very able children and given them valuable insight into the capabilities of such pupils.[1] It therefore seemed desirable to create opportunities for more teachers to participate in similar courses. Not only would the teachers prepare curriculum extension projects but they would also teach groups of very able children, witness the reaction of the pupils and evaluate their work. Gradually, the extension projects would be refined and made available to other teachers for use in the classroom. In this way, not only would teachers gain personal understanding and experience of dealing with very able pupils, but they could eventually become catalysts in their schools, sharing their knowledge with their colleagues. In addition, very able pupils would be given opportunities to work with each other, so experiencing greater challenge than was possible in most classrooms.

It was essential that teachers should be closely involved in the development of identification strategies, curriculum extension projects and courses so that growth would stem directly from their perceptions and needs and be closely related to practical classroom activities. New ideas and techniques should grow from the existing system because teachers acknowledge, understand and sympathize with the need for change and are involved in both the planning, the execution of the plans and the evaluation. Consequently, the first year of office was largely spent developing teacher awareness and cooperation with the reassurance that concern for exceptional children did not mean segregation, élitism or regression to labelling and rigid streaming. This laid the foundation for the following years and helped to establish a common understanding of aims and objectives.

The following chapters are based on the work that developed through in-service education, teacher workshops and curriculum extension courses which were held throughout the county at teachers' centres, in schools and in residential centres. Part One concentrates on how to identify very able children and highlights their special needs. Part Two considers how to provide for those needs, with an emphasis on planning curriculum extension projects. The Appendixes are detailed accounts of how practising teachers have worked with very able pupils from infant to secondary level. Where case histories and quotations are used, real names have been withheld.

Although this book is set in the context of work which has been developed in Essex, its recommendations are relevant to all educators. The problems of identifying potentially very able children who are not high *school*-achievers, or who do not fit into the expected role of scholarly and academic-oriented pupils, are universal. The difficulties of striving to make provision for exceptional pupils are common to many teachers. The needs expressed by exceptionally able pupils and their parents are not generic to Essex but common to many parents and pupils.

Reference
[1]See Appendix A for details of the curriculum extension courses.

PART ONE
Identifying Very Able Pupils

Chapter 1

What do We Mean by 'Gifted' Pupils?

Before we discuss the needs of 'gifted' pupils and their teachers, we need to define and clarify what the term means. When teachers talk of 'gifted' children, two extreme views may sometimes be presented. Firstly, a teacher might say: 'All the children in my class are gifted.' If by this she means that every child has worthwhile attributes, a variety of different strengths or talents, then we could agree. Each child is as important as another and needs an appropriate education. Every child has a contribution to make to the group, something to *give*, something to share. Another teacher might say: 'I have taught for twenty years and I have never met a *gifted* child.' If by this the teacher means that she has never met a young Gauss or Einstein, then again, we would agree that such genius is rare.

The term 'gifted' is also, unfortunately, subject to misconception, and laden with emotive and political overtones. There is a myth that gifted children automatically survive and triumph; that the gift will miraculously manifest itself despite hardship or deprivation; that the 'gift' exists almost separately as a force in itself. The emotive and political overtones derive from terms such as 'privilege' or 'élitism', and the fear of developing special educational provision which gives even greater advantage to those already apparently well endowed.

Consequently, I prefer to use the term 'very able' and would stress that provision for the very able should be seen as an *aspect of provision for all children* – as an integral part of the ideal of striving towards equal opportunity for all pupils. Providing equal opportunity, however, does not mean sameness; not all children can, or need to, learn the same things in the same way at the same time. Nor is concern for the exceptional child to be seen as synonymous with 'labelling'. The teacher's professionalism lies in continuously *assessing* the strengths and weaknesses of each child and then promoting the strengths and strengthening the weaknesses.

I use the term 'very able' to denote a child who has outstanding potential or ability in any one area or in several areas so that s/he needs more than the teacher usually provides in the way of extension activities and resources. There are several aspects of exceptional ability which need recognition:

1 Physical talent
2 Skill in visual and performing arts

2

3 Mechanical ingenuity
4 Leadership and social awareness
5 High intelligence.

An essential characteristic permeating each aspect is creativity.

1 Physical talent

A paradox exists in that outstanding potential is recognized and accepted in certain areas more than in others. For example, a child who demonstrates physical talent is very lucky because s/he is selected for the school team, is allowed to train with other equally talented children, often has special coaching after school, gives public performances and receives the appropriate acclaim. Badges, trophies, colours are awarded to rounds of applause; parents are only too happy to discuss their child's activities; educators are content to provide physical education *according to the needs* of their pupils, encouraging differentiation and specialization; the peer group supports and hero-worships the skills and talents of their contemporaries; radio and television feed society's appetite for demonstration of excellence in all areas of physical talent. Sport is seen to cut across social and cultural barriers and, therefore, is not seen to be divisive or élitist.

A secondary pupil writing about his personal needs said:

I enjoy reading, mostly science fiction. I don't like sport. I find that in school too much emphasis is placed on football matches and colours are awarded to children good at sport. Children who are good academically don't get colours or similar awards, and are often called names which give them an inferiority complex.

2 Skill in visual and performing arts

Pupils with exceptional ability in the creative arts are somewhat less fortunate. Although schools, particularly primary schools, have increasingly developed the creative arts as an integral part of the school curriculum, there are a number of problems which prevent or inhibit young people with considerable talent in music, art or drama from ever realizing their full potential.

For many pupils, often from poorer or culturally deprived homes, the only opportunity they have to discover if they possess ability in any of these areas is provided in schools. In times of economic restraint, resources and facilities for these activities are often curtailed, and it is obviously easier for wealthier parents to provide extra-curricular activities through private lessons, concerts or exhibitions. Moreover, if education is seen by parents in mainly vocational terms, many understandably encourage their children to take secondary courses which have an obvious and practical influence on future employment opportunities. A career in the field of music, art or drama is usually considered to be more precarious than a career in science, computer science or engineering. Parents who have worked hard all their lives to maintain a basic standard of living naturally urge their children to aim for a reasonably secure job with a regular income. Nor have such parents the means to support their children as young, struggling artists. In addition, the adolescent male peer-group pressure often positively discourages a young man from manifesting talent through the creative arts, if such expression does not conform to the stereotype of their sub-culture. During curriculum extension courses, it is not uncommon for a young creative artist to say that he keeps his poetry or love of music secret, or that he deliberately plays rugby so that he is accepted as an artist, or that he was discouraged by parents, teachers and friends from pursuing further study or a career in the creative arts.

3 Mechanical ingenuity

In contrast to this often negative attitude towards the creative arts, one would think that children who are talented in the field of mechanical ingenuity would fare better. However, at primary school level it is, unfortunately, rare to see children making working models, inventing 'machines' or devising 'Heath Robinson' gadgets. Teachers, largely because of their academic background and training, are more at ease in the world of books, promoting verbal or written activities. They express fear of their inadequacy and lack of experience and knowledge in an area which requires technical and scientific expertise. Nor is it unfair to say that at secondary level the field of design/technology has been neglected. The tendency has been to encourage the most able pupils to pursue the traditional university entrance requirements. Three A levels in physics, chemistry and biology, for example, have often been pursued with little application to industry and technology. The courses which are related to design/technology, such as woodwork, metalwork and technical drawing, have too often been regarded as mainly suitable for the average and less able, even then, there has been little opportunity for creative design and technology linked to problem-solving in either the context of this century or the next. Fortunately, this situation is gradually improving as new courses are being designed which incorporate science and technology into syllabuses designed to promote creative thinking, problem-posing and problem-solving. Also there is increasing encouragement for girls to venture into what has always been a predominantly male-oriented activity. If we consider that pupils in our schools in the 1980s are living in a technology age, then educators must:

determine what skills and talents all pupils need;
decide what educational experiences will promote those skills and talents;

identify and cater for the most able who will become the leaders and innovators in the field.

4   Leadership and social awareness

Another ability which needs consideration is leadership and social awareness. Of course *all* pupils should be led towards:

1   an appreciation of personal rights and obligations;
2   an awareness of society and their role within it;
3   an understanding of local, national and world politics.

Some pupils, however, express an unusual empathy, an almost intuitive awareness of the needs of others, a natural understanding and mature appreciation of the issues involved. They are often the natural leaders to whom other children instinctively respond or turn for help. If such children use their talents in the way society condones, then they are rewarded and praised. Sometimes, however, such young people use their talent for leadership in an apparently *negative* way, to protest, defy and question society's standards and traditions. While not suggesting that all such 'rebels' may be harbingers of a new and perfect society, certainly some young people do have a new vision, or at least an awareness of the unjust, irrelevant or blinkered tradition of the adult world. They will, if we allow them a voice, force us to question and seek to justify *why* and *what* we do as parents, teachers, politicians, citizens.

As we develop larger institutions and bureaucracies, the greater is the tendency for such mass organizations to perpetuate themselves, since any change is inevitably slow and the creative thinker is often perceived as the rebel who upsets the *status quo*. Is it not more comfortable to promote the well-behaved conformist who will maintain the well-ordered institution, than to risk the challenge and possible disruption of the innovator? Yet it is the questioner, the innovator, the strong leader, who will lead society towards change, and, surely, it is the obligation of the parent and teacher to be sufficiently mature and humble first to listen and then, hopefully, to arbitrate between opposing needs, values and ideals.

5   High intelligence

The final category of exceptional ability is, perhaps, the most contentious, that of high intelligence. The controversy of genetic inheritance versus environmental influence[1] still continues, but perhaps with greater understanding and acceptance of the inter-relationship of the two. Certainly, an environment which provides varied and stimulating experiences provides rich opportunities for a child to develop the potential he has to grow and to learn; and a child exposed to fluency in language and expression develops a wide range of personal language, an essential tool for communicating and learning. Exceptional ability is, obviously, the synthesis of factors deriving from heredity, environment and opportunity.

Two priorities emerge: firstly, the importance of promoting rich pre-school experiences and the consequent need for guidance of parents of pre-school children; and secondly, the importance of developing rich educational provision for *all* children. Having accepted this, we are still confronted with individual differences of mental ability and, while the teacher should constantly aim at widening experience, presenting opportunities and assessing and encouraging the abilities of all children, she will still be faced with children at each end of the ability spectrum.

What is meant by intelligence?
Intelligence can be discussed in terms of *general* intellectual capacity, and Binet's[2] concept of general intelligence being composed of a number of interrelating factors is as relevant today as it was at the beginning of the century. He classified general intelligence as the ability to:

> reason and judge on the basis of evidence;
> understand meaning and implications;
> maintain a series of ideas logically and consistently;
> adapt and manipulate ideas;
> evaluate and learn in the light of personal experience.

Since Binet's work, other models of intelligence have been suggested;[3] but whatever model of intelligence is accepted, intelligence is a composite collection of mental abilities which enable a child to learn, to think and to deal effectively with the environment. Undoubtedly, this capacity is greatly influenced by factors such as personality, home and school environment, parental and teacher expectation, experience of success or failure.

Some aspects of the processes and skills associated with and deriving from intelligence can be measured, although most testing can be said to reveal what *has* been learned rather than what *can* be learned. Intelligence testing is generally concerned with the areas of: inductive reasoning, verbal comprehension and fluency, spatial relations, numerical skills, figural comprehension. (Identifying children of high intelligence is discussed, in detail, on pp. 21 ff.)

Creativity
An integral characteristic of any special talent or ability is creativity, if creativity is interpreted as the ability to see the unique solution, the unusual combination, the different pattern, the original approach. Otherwise, an exceptional ability, however practised or polished, is the repetition of mastered skills or established knowledge, a transcription of that which is already known.

So often a child's education becomes largely bound up with acquiring knowledge and demonstrating that the knowledge is remembered by scoring well in tests and examinations. Much of school-based success is, unfortunately, the result of a good memory and an accurate appraisal of what the teacher expects. Expectations and goals guide teacher and pupil through the hurdles and hoops of syllabuses to a finishing line and, while there may be some elasticity and flexibility, the tracks are already laid down and the outcomes largely pre-specified.

While every child is creative in play and fantasy, in invention and innovation, as with all other characteristics, there is a considerable variance in the creative functioning of each individual. Highly creative children tend to be more questioning and challenging than most other children. They are independent thinkers, often rebellious and abrasive in the classroom. They will question authoritative statements; challenge the accepted rules and ideas; choose to do things differently.

Teachers describe many highly creative children as non-conforming, difficult to discipline, unconventional, unpredictable. It would seem that in school these pupils may be the most rebellious and the most demanding, but possibly the most at risk since the more education encourages and rewards conformity and the achievement of pre-determined goals, the more subdued the creative spirit is likely to become.

And yet the future of society depends on the new vision of the creative thinker. Society stagnates unless it is revitalized by ideas and challenges injected by people who can look beyond the traditional and accepted norms.

To sum up: exceptional ability appears to develop from a synthesis of elements derived from genetic factors, environmental influences and presented opportunities which are, in combination, fired by the creative process. However, another common characteristic which goes to make up exceptional ability is personal dedication and motivation. Renzulli,[4] in his retrospective study of adults who were judged to be *exceptional within the society*, identified three common characteristics: above average intelligence, creativity and perseverance.

While acknowledging the importance of recognizing and catering for all talents and abilities, I will concentrate on the needs, identification and provision for pupils of *high intelligence* used in the sense of high mental functioning, although there is such an interrelationship and overlap of abilities that rigid classification is both impossible and undesirable. Thus the reference group of pupils throughout the remainder of the book is the top 5 per cent of the intelligence range, although many case histories and quotations used are those of pupils in the top 1 per cent of the intelligence range.

Within this frame of reference, the following chapter examines the needs of very able pupils, their teachers and their parents, highlighting the problems many of them experience.

References

[1]For a summary of the main points in the 'nature/nurture' debate, together with details of recent research, see:

BLOCK, N. and DWORKIN, G. (1977) *The IQ Controversy: Critical Readings* London: Quarter Books

VERNON, E., ADAMSON, G. and VERNON, D. (1977) *The Psychology and Education of Gifted Children* London: Methuen

[2]TERMON, L. M. and MERRILL, M. A. (1961) *Stanford-Binet Intelligence Scale* London: Harrap

[3]For a detailed study of the concept of intelligence, see:

BRODY, E. B. and BRODY, N. (1976) *Intelligence: Nature, Determinants and Consequences* New York: Academic Press

BUTCHER, H. J. (1968) *Human Intelligence: Its Nature and Assessment* London: Methuen

GUILFORD, J. P. (1967) *The Nature of Human Intelligence* New York: McGraw Hill

SPEARMAN, C. (1927) *The Abilities of Man* London: Macmillan

THURSTONE, L. L. (1924) *The Nature of Intelligence* London: Kegan Paul

THURSTONE, L. L. and THURSTONE, T. G. (1941) Factorial studies of intelligence *Psychometr. Monogr.* 2

[4]RENZULLI, J. S. (1978) What makes giftedness? Re-examining a definition *Phi Delta Kappan* 60, 180–4.

Chapter 2

The Needs of Very Able Children, Their Teachers and Their Parents

Children are born with a natural curiosity and urge to investigate the world around them. Their first five years are characterized by exploration and discovery and, fortunately, many parents soon learn to provide appropriate experiences and to circumvent inappropriate ones! Education should promote and feed this natural curiosity and develop the relevant skills to enhance and facilitate the continuous process of finding out about oneself, the immediate environment and the wider community. Exploration is the first necessary step to understanding and acceptance of ourselves and the world in which we function.

The best of our schools certainly consciously endeavour to provide an education which capitalizes on a child's curiosity, and which facilitates *growth*, at *differential rates* according to individual needs. The best examples of this kind of education are often found in infant schools, where it is more common to find teachers promoting individualized learning programmes and group activities developed within a flexible and integrated programme. It could be argued that infant children are, on the whole, more egocentric and uninhibited than older children and, therefore, *demand* individualized learning experiences, but I would suggest that, all too often, as the child grows older the education system becomes more rigid, inflexible and 'class' based, and the child is increasingly expected to conform to the basic group norms. It is not easy for the teacher to be creative and flexible for she, too, is expected to conform under the pressures of examinations, the fragmented day, the larger institutions. All too frequently, the individual has to tailor his/her needs to fit the organization where ideally the organization should be flexible enough to allow a real differentiation, while at the same time providing a common base.

This is not an attempt to apportion blame largely to teachers or administrators; it is merely an acknowledgment of a situation that has evolved largely as a result of tradition, which often becomes blinkered habit, and economic necessity. The two influences are inter-related; the unwieldy institution tending to perpetuate itself, with teachers so engrossed in day-to-day survival that there is insufficient time for rethinking and planning. Creative planning and innovation need *time* for appraisal, evaluation and change. Economic factors have limited, sometimes to the point of crippling, staffing ratios and resources, two essential factors which facilitate and lubricate the process of indiv-idualizing learning programmes.

In considering the needs of the individual child, it is the small group of children whose needs lie beyond those of the 'average', 'above average' and 'below average' pupils who present the greatest problem.

The needs of very able children

In recent years, there has been increasing concern for minority groups of children who have specific learning needs. This concern has, however, been largely for children who are mentally or physically handicapped or emotionally or socially deprived. As a result special services and special schools have been developed to cater for their needs. However, very *able* children also have special needs arising from their specific abilities, which have been largely overlooked not through negligence but often through lack of awareness or through a misunderstanding of the nature of those abilities. These needs spring from three main sources:

1   A feeling of being different

Many very able children experience a sense of being different: they can feel out of step with their family, their friends and their time. And yet it is human nature to want to belong to a group however small that group may be. Such children need friends with whom they can share ideas, they need to be able to communicate with others in a way that is mutually satisfying and relevant. Fortunately, many very able children have supportive parents who understand this feeling and can provide the necessary counselling and guidance to ease the sense of intellectual isolation. Many also have teachers and friends with whom they can relate and share experiences. However, the following remark is characteristic of the many children who are not fortunate enough to find that support:

'I am the loneliest person on the world because I should really be in the twenty-first century. I'm inventing things now but I have to wait until I'm grown up because no one will listen to me.'

John, aged nine years, has 'invented' a 'time-stretcher machine' and, he says, the worst kind of punishment is to be put into it because then time goes so slowly that you never get into the twenty-first century! He is a lonely, disoriented child who lives in a strange, bizarre world of his own where science, fact and fantasy intermingle. He longs to find a friend, but other children find his conversation confusing and rather overpowering, so John has developed the habit of talking *at* any adult who is patient enough to listen.

Louise, aged seven, feels that no one wants to play with her because no one likes her, and so she seeks excuses for staying in the classroom, asking to tidy up cupboards or bookshelves or generally clear up the classroom. The teacher says that when Louise is playing in a group, she constantly adds new rules and suggests changes to make the game more exciting; consequently, the games becomes so complex that the other children become confused and either revert to the original game and exclude her or accuse her of 'spoiling' their game. In mathematics, when she is playing counting games, she likes to use two dice and after adding the score to halve the even numbers and double the odd, or to multiply by three or four. Louise can see quite clearly how the new game should be played, and so becomes bossy and impatient when the other children cannot follow.

Older children who have attended the Essex curriculum extension courses talk quite freely about their feelings of intellectual isolation and the strategies they have developed in order to be accepted, at least superficially, within the peer group. Many of these pupils are regarded by their teachers as very well adjusted since on the surface, they appear to be coping quite well.

Linda, aged thirteen, while she is reading Shakespeare, which is one of her special interests, has certain television programmes, which she knows her classmates watch, running in the background. She says she gleans enough information to be able to join in conversations and she deliberately refrains from using words she knows other children will not understand. She also makes deliberate speech errors and uses the current slang expressions to try to reduce the sense of alienation she feels. Towards the end of the course Linda wrote:

> I have discovered a lot about myself during the last four days ... at last, I don't feel that I am some kind of exceptional freak. Other people have the same problems as I do: being ostracized by classmates seems to be a common problem amongst us, and attempting to be 'one of the crowd' by speaking the same way and acting the same way as others seems a common remedy.

Brian, an apparently easy-going extrovert boy of fourteen, says he has two lives: his private world of astronomy and physics and his school life. He uses two strategies: he plays football and he tells jokes. In playing football, he says that he gains respect and by telling jokes pupils laugh *with* him and not *at* him. He says that he deliberately underachieves and does the minimum work to get by. His school report showed above average but not outstanding results. He was recommended for a curriculum extension course by a teacher with whom he had a very good relationship and who commented that Brian's humour revealed such a perceptive awareness of human nature that he felt he was 'different'. Brian was assessed as having an IQ over 150 as measured by the Wechsler Scale of Intelligence.

Other pupils, usually the more reticent and reserved children, fail to develop such strategies and withdraw into a private world from which it becomes increasingly difficult to emerge. Of course, we all role-play to a certain extent and accommodate to other people's needs and interests, but we also need to express what we feel is our *true* self, develop our individuality and find joy in communicating with others at a satisfactory level.

Jane, at fourteen, said:

> I am a very deep thinker and spend hours pondering over various books on philosophy, sociology and world religions. I have not yet met anyone who thinks along the same lines as I do, although I came nearer to it on this course than previously. I spend far too much time daydreaming, creating whole new worlds and getting totally lost trying to figure out why, what and when, where and how. ... As a rule I find I cannot get on with people of my own age ... sometimes I feel a bit of a social outcast ... an outsider.

2   *The burden of high sensitivity*

Many very able children are acutely sensitive to the world around them; they have a precocious understanding of adult issues, and a premature intellectual awareness of problems without the emotional maturity to cope with them. As adults, we sometimes feel overwhelmed by the complexity of the world around us. Some children perceive that complexity and, understandably, feel anxious and perplexed. They need special counselling to help them to come to terms with their perceptions, to relieve the anxieties and tensions.

Charles, at seven years of age, could *talk* about world poverty, the rising crime rate, racial prejudice; but he found it difficult to go to sleep because he kept wondering what would happen in the future. He frequently woke with nightmares and was still enuretic. The first priority was to ease the burden of awareness and help him to relax and to laugh and play with the gaiety and irresponsibility usually characteristic of childhood. This was accomplished through the concerted effort of parents and teachers. After discussion of Charles's needs, various strategies were implemented at home and at school to provide Charles with stimulating yet relaxing activities. He participated in curriculum extension courses during which he was able to discuss his fears with other children who could understand and sympathize. Now, at ten, he is still a very serious-minded child who is concerned about world affairs, but he does relax and play. He is still very aware of the complexity of the world but is learning to temper that with humour and a greater understanding and acceptance of the world around him.

3   *Exceptional learning ability*

For many very able children the pace of their learning experiences is far too slow. One can sympathize with a teacher who strives to cope with the diverse needs of thirty pupils ranging from the child who learns very slowly and needs much repetition and reinforcement, to the child who instantly absorbs, retains and can apply his/her learning. Very able pupils rapidly exhaust the resources generally available and have seemingly insatiable appetites for more.

Schools tend to provide fiction and reference books suitable for the *majority* of pupils and, although in recent years provision has improved for slow-learning pupils, there has been far less attention paid to the exceptionally able. Mathematics and reading schemes, for example, tend to include far too much repetitive practice for the very able and far too few extension ideas. While it is easy to say that teachers should adapt such schemes to suit the needs of each child, a teacher cannot always be flexible if the resources are not readily available. Nor can she easily contrive, create or conjure resources to satisfy the needs of the very able child.

Hence, such a child spends a great deal of time repeating and practising skills already mastered, and a sense of frustration and boredom begins to develop. In addition, such a child often thinks much faster than s/he can write, and consequently written work is often untidy, careless and minimal. A further frustration for very able children is the pressure to record each stage of thinking in solving a problem when they grasped the solution immediately. One child often puts his hand up to answer a question before the teacher asks it because, he says, he knows she is going to ask it! We can understand ten-year-old Mary's ambition to invent a machine which will pick up and record thoughts directly from the brain, and we certainly sympathize with another junior-school pupil's wish for an acceleration in mass production of word processors which would revolutionize education! Here are comments from two thirteen-year-old children who attended curriculum extension courses. First, **Janet:**

I have discovered that I am not as mad as I thought I was. A lot of people have the same opinions, thoughts and sense of humour as myself. ... I prefer to work at my own pace. At school, I get fed up waiting for others to catch up ... people don't understand this. ... At school I don't work to my full ability.

Mark said:

I found that it was easier to express your opinions here. ... At school, you cannot use your full vocabulary for fear of being called a snob or being different. It was nice for a change to go at your own pace doing work. At school, I am constantly hindered by people who don't understand the lesson. I felt I got on better with the people here ... and that it was easier to speak among yourselves. Everyone seemed to have the same sense of humour.

These feelings of isolation and frustration are commonly expressed by very able pupils. Some children certainly overcome or compensate for these problems, and perhaps that resilience is a gift in itself. Usually, the children who do overcome such problems have within their environment *at least one* alleviating factor. Such a factor might be supportive, relaxed and understanding parents; a culturally rich and stimulating home and/or local environment; a lively, interesting and sensitive teacher; or a supportive peer-group, however small.

The most vital sustaining factor is obviously the home background. Where parents seek to provide adequate stimulation and cultivate opportunities for talking, the child can develop wide interests and openly discuss any frustrations or difficulties s/he encounters. Encouragement and understanding, however, are quite different from pressurizing the child to satisfy parental expectations rather than his/her current interests and needs. A sense of humour and a generally relaxed and caring family atmosphere – or indeed the reverse – is inevitably communicated to the child. Where there is tension or pressure in the home in addition to problems in school, the degree of anxiety can become intolerable and an obvious catalyst in causing behaviour problems.

Some children satisfy their intellectual and emotional needs by developing an intensive and consuming hobby linked with a family interest, or with someone or something in the local environment. A local history or astronomy society, a curator in a museum, a collection of some kind, a personal study of local geology etc., can totally absorb a child for many years. The richer (in cultural terms) the home and the environment, the more opportunity there is for such a hobby to flourish. Homes and communities which are culturally barren tend to breed discontent and mischief, and foster frustration particularly in very able children who usually have very questioning and searching minds.

In discussion with groups of very able pupils, they often talk of a particular teacher who sustained, supported or extended an interest. Such a teacher – someone who is sympathetic, who will discuss ideas and explore new avenues – can be a source of inspiration. Often the teacher's subject is relatively unimportant; the important factor is that she is someone with whom the child can communicate.

The final alleviating factor – a group of like-minded peers who will provide not only a forum for discussion but also mutual support – is the one for which most very able children express a need.

To summarize: very able children do not survive just because they are exceptionally able. They, just as much as other children, have specific problems – which may be intellectual, social or emotional – which need to be recognized. They also need appropriate learning experiences which will sustain motivation and bring personal challenge, excitement and satisfaction. They need opportunities to work and play not only with chronological peers but also with intellectual peers in order to bring them the same personal joy that musicians or footballers, for example, have in playing and working together. They may need counselling to alleviate the pressures which may be caused by precocious awareness of adult issues and a heightened sensitivity to the world around them.

The needs of teachers

Do very able children need exceptionally able teachers? If by exceptional teachers we mean exceptional educators, then *all* children need exceptional educators; teachers who understand the process of education and who are committed to improving the quality of the process rather than judging their educational goals purely by the end product. All pupils need teachers who are catalysts and facilitators, highly skilled in identifying their pupils' needs and in providing appropriate experiences and resources. Such an ideal is unlikely to happen all the time; teachers are prone to the same frailties as other human beings. Only teachers can fully appreciate the demands of a class of thirty pupils with diverse needs, the intensity of activity and personal commitment demanded, and the fatigue of Friday!

However, the teachers of very able children must realize that these children need as much teaching, inspiring, guidance, reassurance and praise as other children do. They do not automatically succeed because potentially they are very able; they cannot always get on by themselves.

After a curriculum extension course, **Susan,** thirteen years of age, wrote:

My main feeling about the course is one of encouragement. I've been encouraged by the fact that there are a lot of people with the same frustrations as myself – *and* that there are a lot of teachers who care about us and are helping us get along. I used to think that most teachers just cared about people who were less bright and always wanted to help them. They think we can get along perfectly well without any help. It's been really great knowing they care about us too.

good point

If by exceptionally able teachers we mean 'subject' experts, then certainly there are times when an exceptional child needs contact with an expert. Teachers may be able to provide resources for pupils to work independently, but this does not offer the excitement of exploring and developing ideas with someone who has a depth and breadth of specialist knowledge and experience. However, the art of good teaching is mainly the art of asking good questions: not closed questions with prescriptive answers, but open-ended questions which stimulate exploration, discussion, creative thinking, problem-posing and

open-ended questions

problem-solving. The best teachers are:

> Men who think as they talk, rather than recall; who speak from the wealth they have learned, rather than from what they have been taught; who argue with a clear recognition and sensitive acknowledgment of the position from which they argue; men who differentiate faith from fact, and label each accordingly; men who in one breath shake not only the conviction but its reasoned base – such are the teachers for youth who are critically and analytically disposed.[1]

Maker[2] suggests that teachers of very able pupils should be flexible, creative, self-confident, with a love of learning and exploration. In addition, she advocates that the teacher should be a 'change agent', who encourages pupils to value and accept the processes of experimenting and the consequent tension of risk-taking and uncertainty.

Torrance[3] stresses that teachers who effectively foster creativity are sensitive to environmental stimuli and possess flexibility of ideas. They encourage their pupils to test each idea systematically and deliberately create situations which require creative thinking.

The teacher of very able children needs the maturity to accept a child with possibly a higher potential than herself, who will sometimes challenge and even threaten the teacher's own knowledge and feeling of security. This challenge can be met if the teacher accepts the role of co-learner with the pupil; a senior learner with a wider experience of life, certainly, but who accepts the shared exploration of new areas and ideas. This joint exploration can bring uncertainty, particularly if the teacher sees herself in complete authority in the classroom and as the main source of knowledge.

The teacher also needs to be a good organizer and classroom manager, committed to promoting group and individual activities whenever possible. Flexibility in the classroom is both the keynote and the product of a teacher's whole approach to education, stemming from her recognition and acceptance that she has a group of children who are individuals rather than a homogeneous unit. In a classroom where the emphasis is on class teaching and strict adherence to the scheme or syllabus, how can a teacher meet the needs of the exceptionally able? An exceptional child needs a different *pace and depth* of learning experience and the teacher must therefore be willing to break the lock-step of the curriculum.

The atmosphere developed in the classroom is equally important. If each child is valued for whatever contribution s/he can make to the community, if each child has moments of success, recognition and praise, then it is much easier to allow individual differences to emerge, to allow the exceptional child to be different yet still a valued member of the group.

Teacher training

While initial teacher training can only be an introduction to the theory and practice of education, all too frequently the topic of 'exceptionally *able* children' receives the minimum of time and attention so that young teachers begin their careers with little or no awareness that such children possibly need special help, even if they are aware that such children exist. So few teacher trainers have had experience of *working* with very able children that little first-hand experience can be shared. The same applies to in-service education where few local education advisers have first-hand experience of such children. The almost universal response from teachers participating in a course has been one of surprise and sometimes guilt because of a new awareness and understanding, a feeling that some pupils have been overlooked, a recognition that very able children do exist and have special needs. Teachers, therefore, during their initial training, need to be made aware that the group of 'children with special needs' not only includes children with behaviour problems, learning difficulties or physical or mental handicaps, but also very able children. In-service education courses which continue to develop teachers' skills and understanding should include courses specifically on the very able child as well as courses on the teaching of reading, or mathematics or environmental studies, etc.

Yet, however aware and sensitive the teacher is, she needs *resources*. Her questioning techniques alone cannot provide extension activities; there must be suitable books – reference and fiction – available, and adequate materials for the children to use. She also needs *support* from: the headteacher who will encourage and allow flexibility and innovation; the School Psychological Service, which will advise on problems which might arise; and, if possible, from an adviser with experience in the field of gifted education.

The needs of parents

When very able children have attended Essex curriculum extension courses, their parents have filled in detailed questionnaires about their children's pre-school development. Most of these parents described their children's pre-school years as generally happy and quite 'normal'. However, some parents had experienced problems such as their child needing little sleep, being very active, difficult to manage, intensely curious, very demanding or 'different' from other children. Whatever the *causes* of these and other behaviour problems might be, these parents, without exception, said that they needed help but had difficulty in finding it.

Many of these parents had no knowledge of the National Association of Gifted Children,[4] but since they did not think their children were gifted, they said that they would not have recognized the Association as a possible source of help anyway.

Stephen's mother, for example, said that he was a very active baby and, when she attended the local clinic, he stood out as the noisiest and most ebullient child. When he began to walk, he was 'into everything' and became very angry when prevented from pursuing an activity. She felt *inadequate* and blamed herself for her apparent mismanagement of this 'naughty' child. Stephen was identified as an exceptionally able child by his first-year junior teacher. She recognized that Stephen's ebullience was the driving force of a searching curiosity. His constant inattention was partly the result of a divergent mind which wanted to explore several avenues at the same time and partly the result of his immediate understanding and retention of what was being said. The family was an ordinary 'working-class' family, Stephen's mother had no expectations or pre-conceptions of the behaviour of an 'exceptionally able child'. She had left school at the end of her fourth year of secondary education, had married a semi-skilled worker at eighteen and Stephen had been born the following year. In a discussion about Stephen, examining both his needs and theirs, his parents described their sense of relief since their feelings of guilt and personal inadequacy were assuaged and they were beginning to understand why Stephen behaved as he did and how they could begin to give him the support he obviously needed.

Sometimes, as the child grows older and extends his/her interests into areas quite different from the parents' own knowledge and experience, a feeling of *intellectual* inadequacy may emerge. One mother very poignantly said, 'We always knew he was interested in unusual things and we tried to help but we didn't know anything. We wanted to help because we didn't want to lose contact with him.' This sense of intellectual alienation can be very distressing both for parents and their children. Parents often realize their own lack of education and their children face the dilemma of functioning in a world quite different from that of their parents.

Some parents whose children required very little sleep discussed the problems this caused in their marital and general family relationships. Sheer fatigue made them increasingly tired and irritable so that tempers flared quickly and patience was in short supply. Consequently, the ensuing tension was communicated to the child or children and the problem was exacerbated.

Sometimes family problems arise because a younger child outstrips an older sibling, and jealousies and rivalries develop when the older child feels less able or inadequate. One mother with three young sons, the youngest of whom she described as 'very quick on the uptake', described a typical incident. The parents had bought a family game for Christmas. The youngest son had read and understood the rules while the two other brothers were still struggling through the first reading. The attempts of the youngest brother to explain to the others were received with anger and frustration. It is quite easy for an onlooker to suggest that the youngest child should learn to be patient and not to interfere, or that parents could possibly have managed the situation more tactfully, but the six-year-old who could see the way forward was excited at the prospect of playing a new game and was irrepressibly 'helpful' in his anxiety to get the game started.

While most parents of very able children manage to maintain a healthy balance between opportunities for work and play, counselling is sometimes needed because parents have such high expectations of a child that there is excessive pressure on him/her to 'achieve'. Perhaps the parents feel that they have failed to fulfil personal ambitions or, indeed, were not given the opportunity to fulfil their own ambitions and, consciously or unconsciously, see the child as a means of vicarious satisfaction.

Sophie's home experiences had been so carefully structured with 'academically'-oriented activities that when she started school, all she wanted to do was to 'play' in the Wendy house and with the sand and water. Her parents were concerned that she was not 'working' and would lose her 'brightness'; her teacher was concerned to provide Sophie with what she obviously needed at that time – a chance to play with other children. Such a situation needed sensitive handling since both parents and teacher had the 'child's interests' in mind, but the 'interests' grew from different aims and values. The most important guide to the solution was Sophie herself. What did Sophie need at that time in her life in order to enable her to function happily and effectively?

'Counselling for balance and effective living' is, perhaps, an appropriate phrase to describe the overall aim of any discussion between parents and teachers about the needs of very able children. However, what would bring about balance and harmony for one child may be quite different from that which would achieve it for another.

Although some parents might be inclined to over-pressurize their children towards premature and narrow academic success, most parents want to see their children happy and enthusiastic about learning. Parents need to be able to talk openly with a teacher when they feel that the child is under stress, without the teacher feeling either threatened or that the parents are interfering. Education should be a triangular negotiation whereby parent, child and teacher express their needs, interests and aims, and a compromise is achieved in the best interest of the child. Parents have a right to be deeply involved in the education of their children; teachers should have the professional competence and maturity to be able to justify what they do, yet respect and acknowledge the parents' wishes and criticisms; children deserve and have a right to an education which is personally motivating and relevant.

References

[1]Ward, cited in NEWLAND, T. E. (1976) *The Gifted in Socio-Educational Perspective* New Jersey: Prentice Hall

[2]MAKER, C. J. (1975) *Training Teachers for the Gifted and Talented: A Comparison of Models* Reston, V.A.: Council for Exceptional Children

[3]TORRANCE, E. P. (1962) *Guiding Creative Talent* New Jersey: Prentice Hall

[4]The National Association for Gifted Children (NAGC) was established in 1966 to provide support and information for teachers and parents.

Chapter 3

Teacher Attitude and Teaching Style

Any theoretical discussion of identification must be linked with the recognition of the need to develop practical identification techniques which the teacher can use in the classroom. However, there is no single technique by which the teacher can be certain that she has fully identified the strengths and weaknesses of any child; but by a combination of careful sensitive observation and objective assessment, a teacher can build up a detailed picture of a child upon which confident judgment can be based. Children develop unevenly. Some 'gifts' require life experience and maturity, and talent of any kind manifests itself only if appropriate opportunities and challenges are presented, hence, the most important factor in the process of identification is that of *provision*.

Teacher attitude and teaching style

The quality and sensitivity of methods, practices and experiences initiated in the classroom will inhibit or encourage the development of individual differences. In classes where teachers work to the 'syllabus' or 'scheme', where every child travels along the same track, there is obviously less opportunity for a teacher to identify individual differences or for a child to reveal exceptional ability. The teacher's teaching style and questioning techniques can *encourage* creative thinking, exploration, problem-solving, discussion of ideas, or *inhibit* pupil response by imposing set expectations, pre-determined goals or conclusions. Observation of a child's abilities should therefore start with the question: 'Does the school and class environment provide the maximum opportunity for each child to show his/her talent? The teacher who strives to promote creative thinking, who is sensitive and perceptive, who is committed to promoting individual and group work will consequently have a greater insight into individual potential.

The personal relationship the teacher builds with each child is very important. All children respond in an atmosphere of love and trust, and a highly sensitive child will be particularly aware of the teacher's attitudes and degree of openness and acceptance of his/her ideas.

Case studies

The following case studies reflect and underline the influence that teacher-attitudes and teaching styles can have on very able pupils. The

21

children's writing also illustrates the level of vocabulary, grasp of syntax and quality of ideas of such young pupils.

Peter (7 years and 2 months)

Peter was identified as exceptionally able in his infant school since at six years he had a reading age of 12+ with comparable comprehension ability. The educational psychologist assessed his ability as 140+ on the Wechsler Scale of Intelligence. At home, he was reading widely and was fully conversant with writers like C. S. Lewis, Edward Lear and J. R. R. Tolkien. He understood and was able to manipulate basic number concepts with ease and enjoyed puzzles, codes and strategy games. He was already bilingual (the second language was German), he had devised his own secret language, ran a savings bank for family, friends and neighbours, giving loans and making a profit even though most people had accounts only in the range of 50p–£1.00!

When he moved into his first junior class, the teacher prided herself on her quiet, well-ordered class. The tendency was towards class-teaching and set class exercises, stars being awarded for neat, completed work. All children worked their way through the maths, English and reading schemes, and their progress was recorded accurately and regularly.

Gradually, Peter began finding excuses for not going to school; he had tended to have mild asthma attacks as a pre-school child and these began to recur with greater intensity. When he was at school, his work was very careless, untidy and incomplete. He was inattentive, daydreamed and was sometimes rebellious. Extracts from his mathematics exercise books reveal the quality of the challenges being set and his response to them (see Fig. 1, p. 23).

His 'mathematics' work is dull and repetitive; there is no exciting problem-solving or exploration of concepts. The work is mechanical computation practice with no practical work and little, if any, relevance to everyday life. (See Appendix B for a description of creative problem-solving activities in mathematics.)

In language, he obviously began by wanting to please his new teacher. On the first day of the new term in September, his work looked presentable; by November, it had deteriorated dramatically (see Fig. 2, p. 24). It is not at all difficult to understand the deterioration when we remember Peter's personal reading experience and level of understanding.

The child's frustration is obvious; the tasks are dull, repetitive and stifling. In discussion with the teacher, she felt that Peter had first to be neat and tidy before he deserved to be given 'different work' and, moreover, the other children would see him apparently being rewarded for 'poor work'. She also felt threatened, and therefore resentful, since a change in her classroom routine meant new approaches, different techniques and greater flexibility.

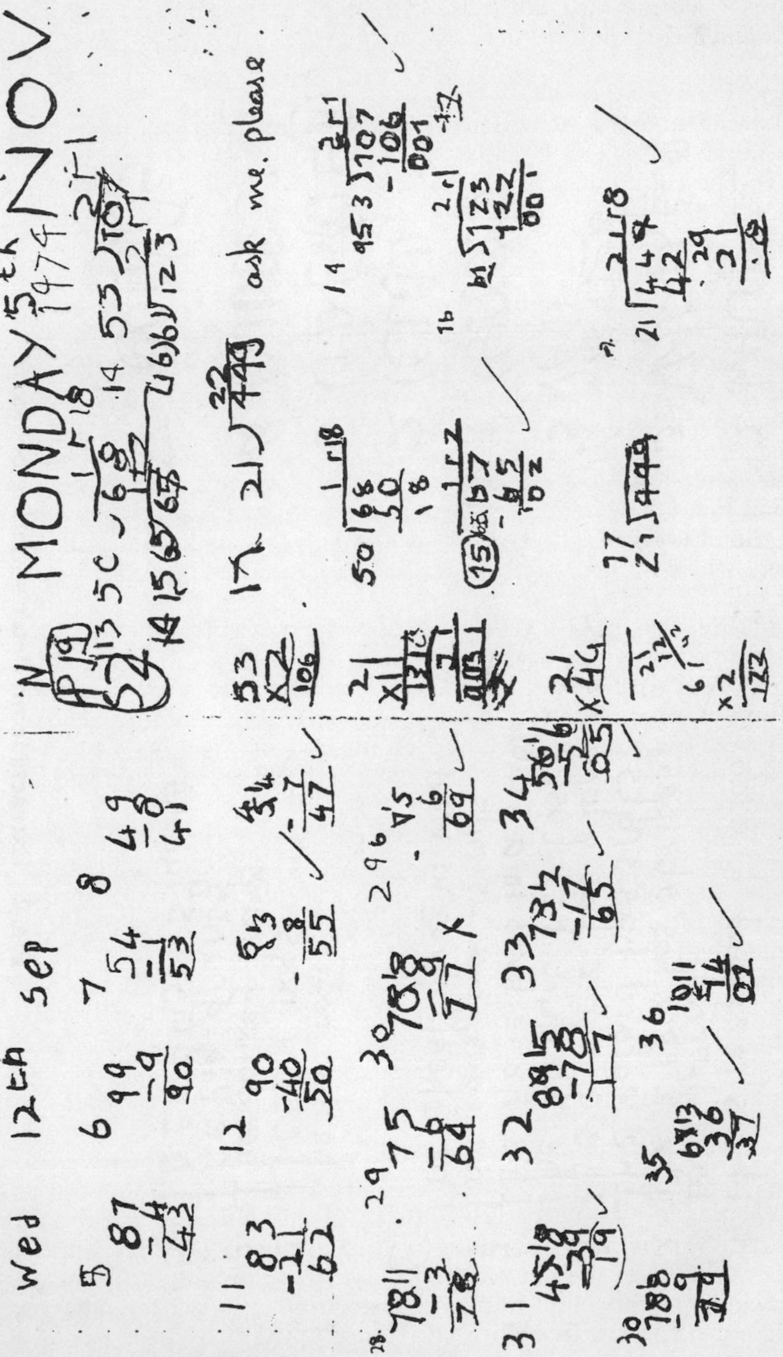

Fig. 1   Extracts from Peter's mathematics books

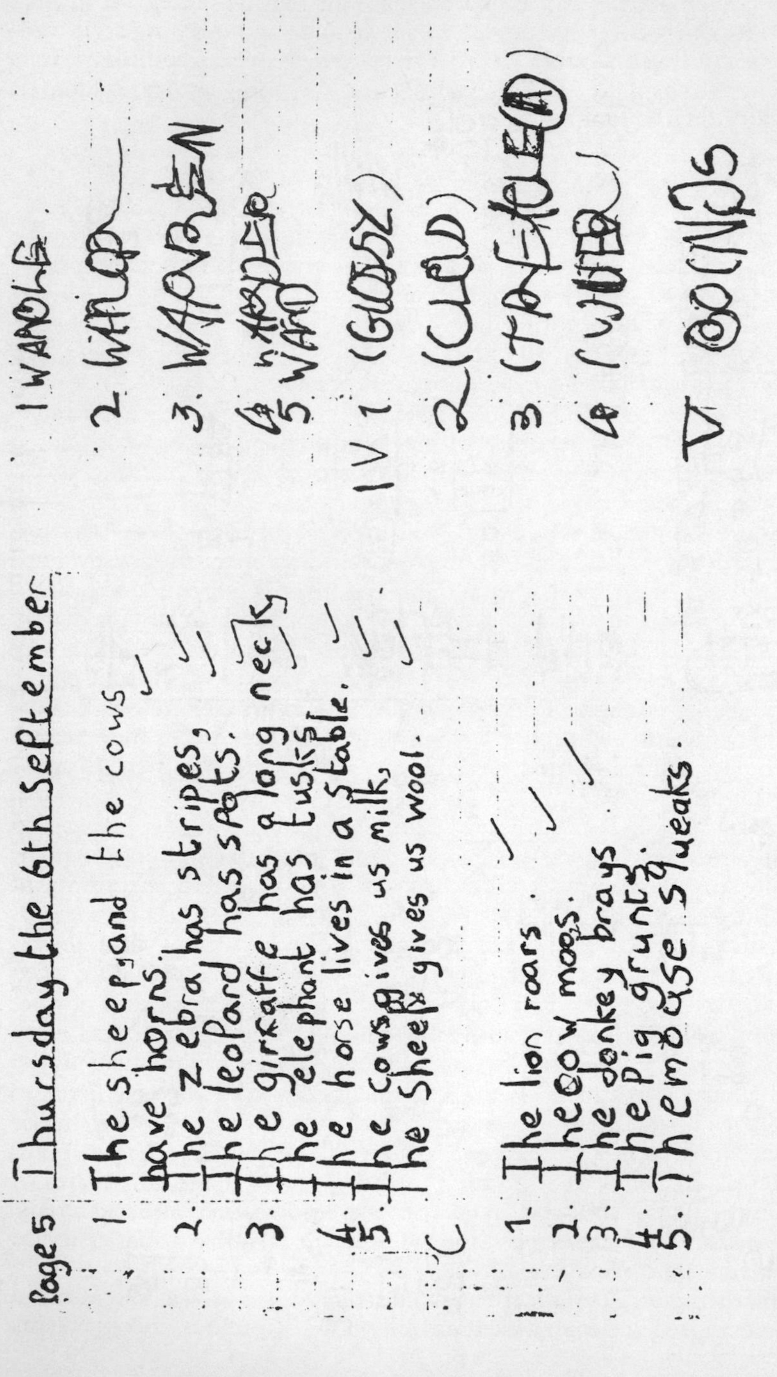

Page 5   Thursday the 6th September

1. The sheep, and the cows have horns.
2. The zebra has stripes, the leopard has spots.
3. The giraffe has a long neck, the elephant has tusks.
4. The horse lives in a stable.
5. The cow gives us milk, the sheep gives us wool.

C
1. The lion roars.
2. The cow moos.
3. The donkey brays.
4. The pig grunts.
5. The mouse squeaks.

1 WANOLE
2. WIILD
3. WAVOREN
4. WANDER
5. WAND

IV 1 (GOODS)
2 (CLOD)
3 (TRESTLE(A))
6 (WIDER)
△ BOUNDS

Fig. 2   Extracts from Peter's writing books

After much debate, and in order to ease the tension, Peter was given a new start with a different teacher whose attitude and teaching style were more creative and flexible. He began to attend school willingly. In a different atmosphere, Peter wrote the following story which is reproduced without alteration:

THE COMPETITION OF THINGOMYGIG

Long ago before you were alive, there lived a little boy called Andrew, who had gone in for the Competition of Thingomygig, where you have to think of what a thingomygig is. This particular boy, Andrew, thought a thingomygig was a rather odd looking creature, that looks rather like a door. Almost a year later when Andrew had forgotten all about the competition of thingomygig, a messenger rapped on the door of Andrew's house and gave Andrew a gigantic parcel, Andrew read the letter which was stuck on the parcel it said 'Dear Andrew winner of Thingomygig competition. Your present which is inside this very parcel is very exciting and we hope you will enjoy it'.

Andrew opened the parcel and to his surprise there was a thingomygig. It had a tall shape, one thin leg, one arm, one eye, a mouth, a nose and was a very small creature. It hopped along, ate boiled bread and drank oil. Andrew kept the thingomygig and called it Raadorn. Raadorn loved telling 'peoms', a 'peom' is a frightening joke thing (here is an example 'on eda yachu rchf elld own') he told them to us day by night until he died. Raadorn lived for twenty years, Andrew was then thirty, he then held a funeral at his house. All his friends came because they were sad at the death of Raadorn.

Peter's new teacher was organized so that pupils worked in groups or on individual assignments. She carefully tried to match the ability of the child with the demands of the task. As far as Peter was concerned, she first discussed with his parents what Peter had read, what he was interested in, what they felt his problems were. She then talked with Peter about his interests and hobbies and built up a relationship of trust with him, as indeed she did with all her pupils. The first practical move was to borrow reading books and reference books of sufficient depth and challenge for him from the central library. She allowed Peter to tape-record his thoughts about the books he read or just to talk to her or to other children in a reader's workshop. She encouraged him to build an interest corner with a group of other pupils on the intricacies of 'Banking'. These children wrote off for information and materials, researched in the local library, interviewed the local bank manager and assembled a superb exhibition.

In mathematics, Peter's interest in strategy games was encouraged and he explored the many inexpensive books of puzzles and problems which are now currently available. The teacher's approach in mathematics was geared to practical problem-solving and exploration of possibilities. Her favourite questions were:

What do you think would happen if . . . ?
Can you find the pattern?
Is the pattern always the same?
Can you discover the rule?
Can you reverse the rule?

Readers will undoubtedly identify such approaches with good primary practice which, of course, is appropriate for all children. However, it is important to emphasize not only the flexibility of organization and approach but the fact that the tasks were challenging and relevant for Peter. Recording was kept to the essential minimum, repetition was avoided, meaningless practice of isolated skills removed. In this particular classroom, children were *expected* to think independently, to talk and work cooperatively, and to produce finished work of a high standard. Catering for Peter's needs had not incurred great financial expenditure nor, in this case, an enormous amount of extra preparation. The major factor was the change in classroom organization, teacher attitude, and teaching style.

James (7 years 3 months)
James, an only child, was a quiet and thoughtful boy who was considered quite bright since he learned easily and readily, retained concepts and quickly acquired skills. He was considered to be well adjusted. He concentrated and completed tasks set, he mixed well with the other children, and played football, although he preferred reading. He also recorded accurately and neatly, made little demand on the teacher, was independent and responsible.

His teacher was concerned, however, because often James drifted off into a world of his own and would gaze out of the window for long periods. Nevertheless he still completed his work. Although he never asked a question, he invariably knew the answer to any question he was asked, even though he seemed engaged in the classroom activity for only a fraction of his time. The teacher felt that she had not really engaged his attention and interest, nor fully occupied, let alone extended, his ability.

She began to talk to him about his interests and outside hobbies and he told her that he liked words and used them to make pictures in his mind. He particularly enjoyed reading poetry, so she began to discuss poetry with him, suggesting poems he might like to read and asking him to introduce her to his favourite poems. The teacher said that initially James was rather shy and reticent but gradually, as he gained confidence and relaxed, he began to write in quite an extraordinary way for a child so young. When he felt at ease and obviously trusted his teacher, he felt able to let her share his thoughts. The atmosphere in the classroom was relaxed and informal, quiet and well organized. Pupils were encouraged to be expressive, each contribution being accepted, discussed and refined in an accepting, non-threatening way. The teacher drew responses from the children rather than imposing her suggestions upon them. Eventually, James's poems were collected into an anthology for other children to read. Here are two of them:

THE SEA
The sea is rumbling, not too soon.
Like a dog licking its food.
Grumbling if it misses its catch.
Then tries again for its mouth.
Slowly invading the seashore
Ever shouting 'more, more, more'.
But on a fine day it eats its food
Throwing the remains behind it to show
It hates the land.

MY CLOUD MOBILE
Above me I see the lands of Heaven
Like a mobile way up high.
Lands of castles, towers and keeps.
Many an ocean, sea of blue
I see towering mountains can you?
Many a hill, valleys too
Mountains still tower then fade away.
Lands keep coming birds keep going
I can never count them one, two, three.
Circles from them come apart.
Circles I can count forty-four or five. Is that right?
My imagination has gone now, I cannot see mountains.

Janet (7 years 4 months)
Janet, an effervescent, dynamic, mature young lady, busied herself in everyone's affairs and often aroused antagonism because she assumed leadership in a rather bossy and even arrogant way. She was very forthright in her opinions and sought the limelight on every possible occasion. She was usually the first to answer and the first to finish, the first to volunteer and the first with suggestions. Her energy seemed inexhaustible and the temptation might easily have been to dam the flood rather than channel and utilize it. Janet's great love was reading; she read aloud with dramatic expression and by seven years of age she had acquired a vast experience of books and could discuss the merits of each with sensitivity and understanding.

Her teacher decided that she could use Janet's expertise as a valuable resource and enlisted her help in selecting and classifying the school library books. Janet wrote stories for other children to read. She reviewed books and read aloud to other classes. She recorded stories for children with reading difficulties and edited a section of the school magazine. She became far less aggressive because she was using her knowledge and ability in real and useful tasks. She had undoubted leadership and organizational ability which could so easily have promoted destructive rather than constructive activities. The teacher had entrusted her with real responsibility and had the humility and sensitivity to realize that the child had considerable knowledge and expertise.

Here is an extract from one of Janet's stories:

MAUG THE DRAGON

Once there was a dragon. He lived in the very cold side of Mercury. He sheltered in a cavern in an iceberg. When the ice blocked the mouth of the cavern he melted it. One day a dragon-hunter came to Mercury. The dragon luckily found some moon flowers while he was looking for somewhere to hide with two friends. They shared them out and ate them. Whatever or whoever eats moon flowers grows wings. It happened to the dragons, as you would expect. They all flew down to earth.

Maug came quickly down on Mount Everest. Some people saw his fire and stayed in their houses, but houses are no defence against dragons and Maug swept down and with a lash of his tail, one of the finest houses in Nepal was down. The dragon stole all the treasure and took it to a cavern in the side of Mount Everest. . . .

He took the treasure back to Mercury. But as he was over Mercury he was hit by a meteorite and injured his wing. When his wing was healed he started looking for a mate. Eventually he chose a mate called Aug, and started trying to get his sperm into Aug's body. This was very difficult because he had to put one sperm in the point of each spike. This took twelve hours, but as soon as he had finished Aug laid the eggs. There were twenty-nine eggs altogether. Maug warmed the eggs, which also helped to start the fire inside the draklings. When the fire was properly inside them the draklings hatched.

While some very able children like Janet can write at length and enjoy producing long stories, others are frustrated because they can think so much faster than they can write, and the problem is exacerbated if the task set is undemanding or repetitive. So much educational achievement is assessed through written recording that many teachers (and parents) feel pressurized to emphasize the development of neat, tidy writing skills. Many very able pupils are reluctant, careless and untidy writers. With such children the teacher needs to *listen* to what they *say*, to the quality of their *thinking*, to the development of *ideas*. Close observation of what the child *does* is important: how s/he approaches problems, how s/he uses ideas and relates concepts.

The following examples illustrate the discrepancy which often occurs between the level of the child's recording and the level of thinking. Significantly, both examples are boys. Girls, on the whole, because of their more mature physiological development plus, all too often, their social conditioning, are more inclined to sit still and to write neatly to please the teacher. Of course, there are boys who also sit still and write neatly, but there is a tendency for more 'reluctant recorders' to be boys than girls.

John, aged nine, drew the following to explain his 'time-stretcher zone'. The picture reveals nothing until one listens to and analyses the quality of John's ideas as he talked whilst drawing. The explanation, a strange mixture of fact and fantasy, is transcribed from a tape-recording.

Fig. 3   John's 'time-stretcher' zone

This is my time-stretcher zone. Say that's the sea and here's the path of orbit. There's a space orbiter here that orbits the earth at the same rate as the earth rotates, so it's always above the same place. Here are two electrodes and it flies really high current right down into the water. Now ... anyone trying to escape from here is dead – in two ways. You see, I say there's two things that are absolutely impossible for anyone to make: a magnet strong enough to pull apart atoms because it would pull apart itself; and absolute zero because at absolute zero nothing can function, which means that electrons cannot rotate around a nucleus, which means they'll go into the nucleus and explode, therefore you can't have absolute zero because the machinery would just get destroyed! Now ... here's the path and if they try to get out here, they're dead – two ways. First, because they'll literally explode because their atoms will stop, and second they'll be electrocuted by the high electric charge. In here ... time is slowed down. Now this is time ... in here. That's a stone and at first it would be going really fast but as it passed through here it would slow down and maybe fall but if it did get through it might really speed up again or it might lose its momentum in the time-stretcher prison or be exploded in the walls. So I'll put a 'boom' there so it's lost most of its mass in the explosion. Another explosion there ... right, so it's only got a teeny-weeny bit of mass left ... because most of its mass has been destroyed, firstly in the explosion as it went in and then in the second explosion as it came out ... so you've got an electrolysed stone and, as it comes down, as it hits the water, you've got a very minute 'sub-sec' time-stretcher zone where time's been destroyed or slowed down. Also, the water in there has risen ... that's the water in the time-stretcher zone. So he (the man) is up there ... in reality in the time-stretcher zone ... because slow time destroys part of the ozone layer and that lets the gamma radiation down destroying part of the atmosphere and causing a vacuum which is lifting the water. It means he (the man) is on a high level and if he tries to get out he's going to be sunk, because he's going to fall down there which, in reality, is a mile, hit the water with such a crash that his boat will fall apart so he is drowned if he tries to escape. So if he tries to escape he is exploded, electrocuted or drowned!

Alan, aged nine and a half, was participating in a curriculum extension course. The project he was engaged in involved a study of the history of man's ideas of the structure of the universe, including those of Aristarchus, Ptolemy, Copernicus, Tycho Brahe and Kepler. Various myths and legends were also studied and discussed and finally the teacher took the children outside to lie on the grass with their eyes closed. They were asked to use their imagination to construct a theory of the universe and when they were ready, to tell their theory to the other children. Alan drew a sketch; the following is an extract from his theory and is transcribed from a tape-recording.

This is my idea of the Earth in about 12 AD, as if I was stranded on an island and I wouldn't have any sense of time but I would have a fair guess that my island was the only piece of land in the whole wide world and the rest was water. I believed that the centre of the world was a gigantic dragon which was running round and round like a hamster in a cage inside and he was panting quite hard so his fire caused the volcanoes and he was beating the inner core out of shape thus giving the effect of tidal waves. His tail beating against the side of the inner core created sound waves and caused earthquakes. The reason he was doing this was that the sun was joined up to the earth by two million kilometres bridges – one called Hades, the metal one that went to the South Pole, and the other Apollo, the one that went to the North Pole. At first I thought, 'I'll sit down and see these little flares coming off the sun. I wonder if they're people trying to cross? Well they must be!' So I thought there must be bridges joining the sun and the moon and the sun and the earth up. And as I said, the dragon in the middle was running around because he thought the sun was going to push in and the earth was going to collapse in as well because the strands would break and thus crush in his world. So he was running round to keep the world steady and the sun and the moon steady. He had to have these massive great stones to equalize the weights of the pushing and pulling thus giving a steady ratio of the moon pulling and the sun pushing. So he had to create a sort of drag effect to equal them out and these were on transparent pillars so you couldn't see them and say 'Ah! that's a give-away.' The moon was also done like that except with transparent harnesses made of strong waterproof metal . . .

The case studies which have been presented illustrate the crucial importance of the teacher's attitude and teaching style in identifying and providing for the needs of very able pupils. The vital factor is that the teacher should be committed to looking for and promoting individual differences in an atmosphere of cooperation and respect for all children's abilities and strengths. The second necessary factor is that the teacher should be concerned with the *process* of learning rather than the *product*, the quality of the pupil's thinking rather than the prescribed goal. Finally, the teacher should be concerned to draw creative responses *from* the child instead of *imposing* set ideas and conclusions.

Chapter 4

The Use of Checklists

Perceptive, sensitive observation by the teacher, together with an atmosphere which encourages individual expression, is the first requirement for identifying an exceptional child. However, the teacher often needs help to refine her sensitivity and to alert her to characteristics which she might otherwise overlook.

During in-service education courses which took place in Essex, the characteristics of very able children were studied using various checklists.[1] The checklists were used initially to stimulate discussion. In a practical exercise which then followed, the 100 teachers who were participating in the in-service courses used the checklists, plus their own subjective observation, to build profiles of pupils in their classes. At the same time, characteristics of the pupils who were participating in curriculum extension courses were being studied by the teachers involved. Those pupils considered to be exceptional were said to have the characteristics listed below. The list is a collective one based on the most common traits observed and is not arranged in a hierarchy. No pupil would portray *all* of the characteristics but a child showing a significant number of them could well have exceptional potential.

Checklist of characteristics of very able pupils

Possesses extensive general knowledge, often knows more than the teacher and finds the usual reference books superficial.

Has quick mastery and recall of information, seems to need no revision and is impatient with repetition.

Has exceptional curiosity and constantly wants to know why.

Shows good insight into cause–effect relationship.

Asks many provocative searching questions, which tend to be unlike other children's questions.

Easily grasps underlying principles and needs the minimum of explanation.

Quickly makes generalizations, can extract the relevant points from complexity.

Often sees unusual, rather than conventional, relationships.

Listens only to part of the explanation, and appears to lack concentration or even interest, but always knows what is going on – when questioned usually knows the answer.

Jumps stages in learning, often frustrated by having to fill in the stages missed.

Leaps from concrete examples to abstract rules and general principles.

Is a keen and alert observer, notes detail and is quick to see similarities and differences.

Sees greater significance in a story or film, and continues the story.

When interested becomes absorbed for long periods, and may be impatient with interference or abrupt change.

Is persistent in seeking task completion; often sets very high personal standards and is a perfectionist.

Is more than usually interested in 'adult' problems such as important issues in current affairs (local and world), evolution, justice, the universe, etc.

Displays intellectual playfulness: fantasizes and imagines, is quick to see connections and able to manipulate ideas.

Is concerned to adapt and improve institutions, objects, systems; can be particularly critical of school, for example.

Has a keen sense of humour; sees humour in the usual, and is quick to appreciate nuances and hidden meanings.

Appreciates verbal puns, cartoons, jokes, often enjoys bizarre humour, satire and irony.

Criticizes constructively, even if sometimes argumentatively.

Is unwilling to accept authoritarian pronouncements without critical examination; wants to debate and find reasons to justify the 'why and wherefore'.

Mental speed faster than physical capabilities, so often reluctant to write at length.

Prefers to talk rather than write, and often talks at speed with fluency and expression.

Daydreams and seems lost in another world.

Reluctant to practise skills already mastered, finding such practise futile.

Reads rapidly and retains what is read, can recall in detail.

Has advanced understanding and use of language, but sometimes hesitant as the correct word is searched for and then used.

Shows sensitivity and reacts strongly to things causing distress or injustice.

Empathizes with others and often takes a leadership role, very understanding and sympathetic.

Sees the problem quickly and takes the initiative.

While the checklist may have been useful in helping initially to sensitize and refine teacher awareness of very able pupils, after discussing and using it in the classroom, the impact was even greater. For although teachers reported back that their awareness of very able pupils had increased, they also said that their observation of *all* their pupils had improved and that they had been far more aware of consciously *creating opportunities* for pupils to reveal these characteristics.

Checklists, obviously, are only useful if a teacher is *allowing* and *encouraging* pupils to manifest these characteristics, and whenever possible teachers need to give specific examples of what the child says and does which will help to crystallize their observation. It is the quality of the teaching and the quality of the experiences being developed in the classroom which allow the pupil to reveal, and the teacher to identify, these traits. Inevitably, therefore, by improving a teacher's skill one is improving the quality of her perception and awareness.

In addition, knowledge of a child's hobbies and out-of-school activities may indicate a special talent or interest and frequent consultations with parents will give them the opportunity to discuss their child's special interests and needs.

Three categories of very able children
Very able children are not necessarily high-achieving children; they may well fall into two other categories: pupils who manifest problems which may obscure their intellectual ability; and pupils who could be described as covertly very able who, while 'doing their stint', refrain from revealing their ability. In the first instance, the teacher's attention may be totally absorbed in coping with the overt problem, and a pupil who is very aggressive, disruptive or inattentive does not fit into the stereotyped picture of a very able child. By contrast, the covertly very able child who can be relied upon to work is often overlooked and taken for granted.

The high-achieving child
High-achieving children usually *identify themselves* by the quality of their responses or activities and so this is the obvious and easiest category of very able children to identify. A pupil in this category is the successful, erudite young scholar – the stereotype of 'the gifted child'. S/he is overflowing with knowledge and astonishes everyone with the profundity of her/his ideas. For example, **Susanne,** at eight years of age, was interested in windmills and aero-space dynamics. On both topics she was very knowledgeable and the quality of her observations, ideas and background information was startling! **Andrew** had studied moths and butterflies and, as a third-year junior child, was able to set up a display for the rest of the school, complete with transparencies, a recorded commentary and detailed background notes. **Rajiv,** a young scholar steeped in Indian mythology and literature, told detailed and lively stories to other children. He also differentiated between Indian religions with a high level of understanding. **Linda,** at eight years of age, asked to learn Latin and Greek since she had read classical stories in translation but would prefer to read them in the original so that she

could make her own translations. She was always fascinated by words and spent a great deal of time browsing through etymological dictionaries. Her favourite books were: Various *Doctor Who* novels; Shakespeare *King John, Richard II, Macbeth, Titus Andronicus, Julius Caesar, Hamlet* and *Othello*; A. C. Clarke *2001: A Space Odyssey*; Homer *The Illiad, The Odyssey*; H. G. Wells *The War of the Worlds*; Agatha Christie *Death on the Nile*; Patrick Moore *Spy in Space*; *The Penguin Dictionary of Quotations*; *The Guinness Book of Records*; *The Exploits of Hercules*; *Handbook of Greek Mythology*; Plato *The Apologies*; Tolkien *Lord of the Rings*; books of humour and mythology.

At eight years of age, she said that she would like to read: Goethe *Faust Part 1 and 2*; Charles Darwin *Autobiography*; *Complete Works of Plato*; Dostoevsky *Crime and Punishment*; Aeschylus *Prometheus Bound, Seven Against Thebes*; *The Complete Works of Euripedes*; *Monty Python and the Holy Grail*.

Michael had always been fascinated by numbers. At two years of age, he could count stairs, cars, anything up to 26, because that was the number of characters on the Mr Men frieze on his bedroom wall. One day his father noticed that he always counted from right to left and suggested he tried from left to right.

'One, two, three – no, I can't!'

'Yes, you can, have another try.'

'One, two, three, four, five. No, I can't, Daddy, because Mr *Strong* is number twelve!'

A few months later, a full-page advertisement of cars on a motorway had him happily counting to 100, and he could frequently be heard saying the numbers quietly to himself.

In his second year at infant school, aged 5 years 6 months, he obviously enjoyed playing with numbers and was frequently heard muttering to himself calculations such as:

'What is half of 53? – $26\frac{1}{2}$.'

'There are 240 seconds in four minutes.'

'Twenty-five years ago I wasn't alive, nor was Graham, (his younger brother) but Daddy was – he was fourteen and Mummy was eight.'

'Nana and Grandad will be here in nine weeks, that's 63 days.'

'In 87 years I will be 92 – in a million years I will be dead.'

He could manipulate large numbers with ease and, for a while, was fascinated with time, converting hours and parts of hours into minutes and then seconds, and vice versa.

These children may be very mature emotionally and also socially well-adjusted, but even if there is a problem, the teacher can identify the exceptional ability because the evidence is apparent.

The child with a behaviour problem
Sometimes, however, a behaviour problem masks the potential ability. The teacher's attention is understandably absorbed by the child's

behaviour, particularly if the child is aggressive, extremely withdrawn, very active or disruptive.

Adrian was so aggressive towards other children that both they and the teacher found it extremely difficult to cope with him. He was inattentive but also demanding. He interfered with other children's work, produced little work himself and gave little evidence of exceptional ability except in the quality of his questioning. He was referred to the psychologist because of his behaviour problems. At this time he was eight years of age and, when tested on the Stanford-Binet Intelligence Scale, had an IQ score of 160+. An interview with his parents revealed that they had separated several years earlier, had subsequently found new partners but had still remained good friends. (Adrian's father picked him up from school each day and took him home.) The causes of the separation had never been explained to Adrian who was confused by the unusual relationship and could not understand why his parents had separated but were still in regular, friendly contact. It was suggested that Adrian's parents should explain and help him to understand their relationship with each other and with him. At school, because of prolonged inattention, he had failed to acquire a sequence of basic number skills and, although his verbal skills and reasoning ability were high, he was a non-writer and a reluctant reader. His vast general knowledge had apparently been largely acquired from television and long conversations with his grandfather, who also read extensively to him. Adrian needed skilled remedial help to develop his reading skills and to enable him to bridge the gaps in the development of certain number concepts and writing skills so that he could perform at levels commensurate with his thinking ability. His parents also needed counselling so that they could alleviate the emotional insecurity Adrian so obviously felt.

However, the problems may not be *obviously* psychologically based. Physical disability arising from psychological distress may mask exceptional potential.

Throughout infant and junior schooling, **Helen,** an only child, had suffered from severe asthma attacks which abated during school holidays and increased in intensity as the term progressed. Despite frequent absence, she coped well with her school work, keeping level with the most able in the class. Her third-year junior teacher noted this and asked for a diagnostic assessment of her ability by the school psychologist. Helen's full scale score on the Wechsler Intelligence Scale was 140+. Interviews with Helen and her parents revealed that she found her classroom very noisy and she said that she could not concentrate. Being a shy and sensitive child, she recoiled from the often exuberant and lively games in the playground. Helen's mother said that her daughter was a perfectionist and often worried about 'getting things wrong' or 'not being able to finish in time'. At home she spent a lot of time in her room reading, and although she had a few faithful friends she enjoyed quiet and solitary activities and, being an only child, was accustomed to a very peaceful and quiet home environment. Her mother said that the anxiety and tension built up until Helen had another asthma attack and was forced to stay at home for several days. Helen had always been a sensitive child and so her mother had accepted this pattern of behaviour, feeling that there was little she could do about it except to be understanding and hope that Helen would 'grow out of it'.

It was difficult to suggest an easy solution since children collectively tend to be noisy and exuberant! The teacher was able to alleviate the problem by sometimes letting Helen and a friend work in the 'quiet' room. She also tried to reduce Helen's anxiety about completing her work by extending the finishing time and by consciously praising and reassuring her about the quality of her effort and of the finished piece of work.

Other problems may arise from a direct physical handicap such as hearing or sight impairment.

David's mother was concerned because he often seemed to be in a world of his own and was generally absent-minded. Eventually she wondered if possibly he did not *hear* what she said. At school, he was considered to be coping well, of average ability and his teacher was satisfied with his progress; but she also agreed that David was prone to lose himself in a book and become quite oblivious to things happening around him. After a medical examination at eight years old, it was discovered that David had a bi-lateral sensorineural hearing loss averaging 35–40 Db in speech frequencies. He was prescribed a post-aural hearing-aid and was required to wear it for most of the time. The educational psychologist assessed him as an exceptionally able child who seemed to have compensated for his aural deficiency by deducing or guessing when he could not quite hear what was being said. When engrossed in an activity David was, like many children, lost in his private world, but was even more oblivious because he was not looking at the person who spoke to him and so did not realize something was being said. A further problem arose because David was very upset at having to wear a hearing-aid; he felt self-conscious and worried about being teased. Parents and teacher needed to be especially understanding and the situation between David and his peers had to be handled with tact and sensitivity.

Sight impairment is, possibly, more easily identified since a great deal of school work depends on fine hand/eye coordination and a child who is clumsy or straining to focus is more likely to be noticed. Also, the persistent headaches which frequently accompany eye strain usually lead to a vision test. However, it is still possible to miss a slight impairment when a child is able to compensate for inaccurate vision through high-level reasoning or deduction.

The covertly very able child
The quiet under-achievers are often shy, reticent children who seldom ask a question because they always understand and therefore have no need to ask. Sometimes they realize that the questions they would like to ask are not like those asked by other children and so they refrain from asking because they do not want to be 'different'. Other such children are too polite to bother a busy teacher, and so when they constantly finish their task before the others, they fill in the time by spinning work out or by decorating it beautifully. Some identify with the problems a busy teacher has and refrain from adding to those problems out of consideration and understanding. Most teachers can identify the group of pupils who quietly get on with any task set, and it is understandable that if most of their attention is given to the slow-learning, disruptive and more demanding children, they have little time left for those who *appear* to need less attention.

A child who produces page after page of neat, correct sums or well-written stories without error may be a 'credit' to the teacher but is still likely to be under-achieving. A child who seldom makes mistakes or *needs* to ask questions is unlikely to be experiencing challenging tasks or problems.

A high proportion of under-achieving *girls* come into this covertly very able category. During the years 1972–82, teachers in Essex were asked to nominate exceptionally able pupils for curriculum extension courses. A total number of 1,330 pupils were nominated: 896 boys (67 per cent) and 434 girls (33 per cent). In numerous workshop discussions on identification, it is very evident that teachers tend to notice, reward and encourage questioning 'deviant' behaviour in boys to a much greater extent than they do in girls.

Social pressures also can inhibit girls from asking too many questions or demonstrating *intellectual aggression* in the pursuit of new ideas. Many parents (and teachers) tend to expect girls to be docile, neat and tidy, well-mannered, considerate and 'ladylike'. While most parents also expect their sons to be considerate and gentlemanly, independent thinking, questioning and challenging behaviour is perceived as *masculine* and acceptable.

During curriculum extension courses most girls, even at primary level, hold back during discussion. They are generally more reticent and reluctant to express their ideas and often their ideas are conventional and predictable. Their work is generally more neatly presented but more prosaic and conforming. With encouragement, which sometimes amounts to *goading*, the girls do express ideas which are creative, challenging and original, but the teacher has to work very hard to change the stereotyped response which is initially given.

A child who has obvious negative feelings towards school may be a covertly very able child. S/he may not fit into the quiet, undemanding, reticent and/or conforming pupil category but instead may appear lethargic, disinterested, apathetic, lazy, difficult to motivate. Work may be superficial, unfinished, and careless until a sudden, unexpected interest is aroused and the pupil surprisingly asks searching, provocative, perceptive questions. Such a pupil might reveal extensive general knowledge about 'non-school' subjects, may have demonstrated 'street wisdom' or 'wiliness' in solving everyday problems. S/he might be very aware of adult problems or show a mature understanding of the world around him/her. Such pupils may be disillusioned and cynical, hypercritical of peers and adults. Boredom and apathy often lead to a state of enervation, low self-esteem, lack of drive, loss of motivation. If the child's home background fails to provide stimulating experience and challenge, the feeling of hopelessness is exacerbated. Many children from poor or deprived homes come into this category.

CHARACTERISTICS OF THE UNDER-ACHIEVER
Vernon summarizes the characteristics of the under-achiever as follows:

> He sees himself as inadequate, has low aspirations, is apathetic and does not enjoy studying; he is poorly adjusted or anxious, or sometimes rebellious against all that school stands for, often low in popularity. Such students tend to come more frequently, though not exclusively, from unstable or broken homes, of low socio-economic backgrounds, where there is little tradition of, or concern for, higher education.[2]

The characteristics of the under-achieving child can also be summarized in a checklist (see below). Such a checklist indicates collective traits and serves to alert the teacher by focusing attention on a number of possible clues which can be further investigated. The traits have been collected from the profiles of 200 under-achieving pupils who have been referred by teachers and parents to educational psychologists who subsequently assessed the pupils as having exceptional potential. The test used for assessment was the Wechsler Scale of Intelligence for Children. Many of these children had higher scores on the non-verbal than on the verbal sub-tests. (This test is discussed in detail on p. 57, together with the significant differences between the verbal and non-verbal sub-tests.)
The underachiever may be:

Generally anti-school and very critical of its values. Often scathing in remarks about teachers and lacking in enthusiasm for most school activities.
Frequently abrasively humorous with an ironic perception of other people's weaknesses.
Orally good while written work is poor and incomplete. He/she is not really interested in seeking the teacher's approval by completing work.

Apparently usually bored and lethargic, lacking energy and motivation. He/she watches the time and is anxious to finish the school day and leave.

Restless, inattentive and easily distracted, often at the root of mischief and practical jokes.

Absorbed in a private world, often wasting time by just doing nothing or distracting other pupils.

Friendly with older pupils, deliberately seeking their company and often accepted by them.

Impatient and critical, sometimes rude and insolent, finding difficulty in making relations with peers and teachers.

Emotionally unstable, very prone to moodiness or bad temper, apparently easily frustrated and lacking in kindliness towards others.

Outwardly self-sufficient and apparently careless or indifferent to school standards.

Irregular in attendance but able to keep up with the other children.

Defensive but very astute in argument and self-justification.

Often the leader of the 'malcontents' and the anti-school group.

Well-endowed with 'low cunning' and survival skills.

Able to manipulate others while not being personally committed or involved.

But, the under-achiever is also:

When interested, inventive and original, although impatient and reluctant to persevere with inbetween stages.

Quick to learn new concepts and able to pose problems and to solve them ingeniously, especially those unrelated to school tasks or 'academic' subjects.

Able to ask provocative, searching questions and very aware of problems about people and life generally.

Persevering when motivated, sometimes performing at a high level in one or two areas only, and particularly when the relationship with the teacher is very good.

Inventive in response to open-ended questions.

Philosophical and wise about everyday problems and commonsense issues.

Perceptive in discussions about people's motives, needs and frailties.

However, while a checklist of characteristics may be a useful tool in helping to refine teachers' observations of pupils, such a checklist is of most value to teachers who are already teaching in a way that allows pupils to reveal those characteristics. Some teachers (mainly from secondary schools) have complained that the checklist is too demanding, that they do not know the pupils well enough to answer the questions. Also, many of the positive characteristics would be revealed by pupils to those teachers with whom they already have a good understanding and rapport, and not to those teachers perceived as less sympathetic or approachable. The checklist of the under-achiever also needs a sympathetic teacher since many of the traits are far from endearing and certainly not usually associated with exceptional ability.

Nevertheless, in teacher workshops the important themes have been:

If this checklist describes the characteristics manifested by very able pupils, how can teachers promote opportunities for pupils to reveal them?

How many pupils manifest the characteristics of the under-achieving pupil?

Chapters 3 and 4 have examined the importance of teacher attitude, observation and teaching style. There has been little attention given to the role of parents in identifying the very able child. Chapter 5 considers the importance of parental involvement and discusses the need for good parent–teacher relationships.

References
[1]The checklists used were those published in:
DES (1974) *Gifted Children and their Education* London: HMSO
OGILVIE, E. (1973) *Gifted Children in Primary Schools* Schools Council Research Studies, London: Harper and Row
RENZULLI, J. (1975) *Scale for the Rating of Behavioural Characteristics of Superior Students* University of Connecticut: Storrs
[2]VERNON, P. E. (1977) *Gifted Children* London: Methuen

Chapter 5

Parental Involvement

Many schools are increasingly involving parents in discussion about their child's education. The increased focus on specific counselling and pastoral care in secondary schools has meant that parents are invited to contact people such as form tutors and heads of year to discuss their child's course options, academic progress, emotional and social problems. At primary level, parents are often encouraged to provide extra assistance in the classroom, in the library, on school outings, so that informal meetings occur more frequently. But it is, perhaps, during a child's infant school education that the most frequent and personal communication occurs.

Many parents and children visit the school beforehand and talk at length with the reception teacher. Mothers often take their young children to and from school so that teachers and parents have opportunities to talk. The best infant schools ask for details of the child's pre-school development – physical, mental, emotional and social growth. This procedure is relevant for all children, but in the case of the most able children, certain characteristics may provide evidence of exceptional potential.

Pre-school profiles
Some exceptional children accelerate through the early developmental milestones: they walk early, show an early awareness of their surroundings, and a precocious inquisitiveness about the world around them. Some appear to require less sleep than most other children: many mothers talk about their young children still being awake at 11 pm and ready to begin the day at 4 or 5 am. Others are very active, demanding children who strive to be independent, expressing extreme frustration when they cannot accomplish a task entirely by themselves

At two-and-a-half years of age, **Tracy's** favourite phrase was 'I can do it by myself!' She constantly refused help and was quite determined to succeed by her own efforts. She had always been independent from a very young age. She sat up at four months, wanted to feed herself at six months and walked at eight months. Her mother had felt quite inadequate because she seemed unable to satisfy Tracy's needs. She used the phrase: 'I could not content her.' When Tracy played with other children, she was the organizer, the one with ideas, the instigator of mischief!

Ian's favourite occupation was taking things to pieces to see how they worked. In the early hours of the morning he would wander downstairs, stand on a chair to switch on the light and proceed to explore and investigate. Mother, a single parent, would frequently come downstairs to find chaos, but an engrossed and contented child busily finding out! Mother visited the local clinic and sought advice about how to deal with her very demanding son. Ian was admitted early to school on the recommendation of the educational psychologist who assessed his IQ as at least140+ (Wechsler Scale of Intelligence). His reception teacher commented on the high level of Ian's activity, the rapidity with which he absorbed and retained any new concept and his insatiable appetite for making 'inventions'. She gathered old clocks, weighing scales, small machines of all kinds, Meccano, toy engines, multifarious bits of 'rubbish' from which he constructed 'gadgets'. The teacher also discussed home problems with Ian's mother, giving advice on activities Ian would enjoy and books he might read.

Striving towards early communication is common and early talking is a general characteristic of exceptionally able children. Even when a child does not begin to talk very early, often when s/he does, the language is well advanced with phrases or sentences being used from the beginning. Frequently, such children ask searching, unusual questions such as:

What holds up the moon and the stars?
Where has October gone?
Why does a light shine?
Why is rain wet?
How did I begin? – Well, you grew in Mummy's tummy ... – No, how did I *begin*? – You grew from a seed ... – No, I know that: what made the seed start to grow in the beginning?
What makes flowers different? Why do they grow? How do they grow? How do I grow?
Why do words come from my mouth?
Why is everything coloured?

Many very able children learn to read early not by being taught but by constantly pointing to a word or phrase and asking, 'What does that say?' They then surprise their mothers by reading a shop sign or newspaper heading. Sometimes they read a favourite story after hearing it and linking the sounds with the words. Even when children do not learn to read before they start school, many accelerate through the early reading stages, requiring little repetition or practice but absorbing the code on impact and quickly reading with expression and understanding.

Systematic recording of a child's pre-school developmental characteristics can yield evidence which may indicate exceptional potential. However, some very able children have a perfectly conventional and normal pre-school developmental pattern, although early language development, perceptive and unusual questioning and the early acquisition of reading skills are very common.

Social workers, doctors in pre-school clinics, playgroup leaders and nursery school teachers should all be made aware of the characteristics which may indicate exceptional ability so that help and guidance can be given to parents when necessary. Many problems can emerge before the child begins school: parents may find such children demanding and exhausting; some children have problems caused by frustration and boredom; some children's inquisitiveness leads to destructiveness; some children know what they want to achieve but lack the manual dexterity to accomplish the task and show their frustration through unusually frequent temper tantrums and tears.

In looking at pre-school development, however, teachers must be aware of the differences in children's pre-school experiences. A child from a secure background where s/he is loved and happy, where parents and perhaps grandparents have given their time and understanding, where conversation has been interesting and stimulating, where books and games have been plentiful, has had many opportunities to discover, explore and grow. For such a child beginning school is an extension of experience which is not very different from home values and expectations. The teacher's language and expectations coincide with those of the parents and the transition is smooth and natural.

In contrast, a child from a home where s/he has felt insecure and unloved, or where s/he has had little stimulus, or where adults have had little time for talking, reading or exciting exploration, will have been deprived of rich and nourishing pre-school experiences. Such a child will not have had the opportunities to discover what s/he can do, and will not have experienced the security which must necessarily underline personal growth and maturity. For such a child, the teacher has to be sensitively aware of the different background, has to work much harder to bridge the gap between home and school, has to present opportunities for exploration and discovery which the child has missed. Sometimes the child's language is limited and the teacher must consciously extend language facility and fluency before the child can express ideas. Such a child may, potentially, be very able.

If the first five years of a child's life are accepted as crucially important to future development, several points for much wider consideration arise. Firstly, parents need to have more guidance centres to which they can refer and discuss problems. All parents might need such support, but many parents of very able pupils have expressed their bewilderment, their feelings of personal inadequacy and even despair when their child has presented problems such as those described earlier. They needed advice and help but seldom found it.

Secondly, all children should have access to exciting and stimulating pre-school experience, but the number of nursery schools and pre-school playgroups (at least in the UK) is grossly inadequate. Often, the children who least need such provision come from wealthier homes where, if the State does not provide facilities, parents can afford to pay for private nursery education. The children who most need such provision tend to come from poorer homes where, if there is no State provision, parents can ill afford to provide it themselves.

The final question for consideration follows on from this point: to what extent can schools compensate for deprivation or lack of stimulus in the home? Exceptional ability needs not only recognition but fostering and nurturing. A very able child from a culturally poor home has obviously to struggle so much harder to succeed than a child from a more privileged or supportive background. The strongest do succeed, often against great difficulties, but many children who are potentially very able, fail to find the understanding and support they need and consequently fail to overcome the difficulties they encounter.

An infant school teacher therefore has a great responsibility not only to recognize a child with exceptional potential but also to begin to meet that child's needs at an early age. She has to bridge the gap between home and school, alleviate problems which may already have developed, advise parents when necessary, and *listen* to parents when the child is unhappy at school.

A child's response to his/her first school experiences leaves a lasting impression, so reinforcing a child's desire to learn through success and satisfaction should be the teacher's constant aim. Many very able children become bored with school after only a few months, and a pattern of under-achievement or a negative attitude towards school begins to develop.

Several groups of Essex infant teachers and headteachers (approximately fifty in all) participated in workshops to discuss what they needed to know about a child when s/he started school, and the best way to gather that information. It was generally agreed that to present most parents with a long and searching questionnaire about their child would be intimidating and rather threatening. Parents, naturally, are keen for their child to settle into school happily and make a good start. Any suggestion that the teacher was pre-judging the child, or making comparisons prematurely, might cause anxiety and apprehension. In some cases, parents might find great difficulty in personally coping with such a questionnaire. Teachers agreed that informal discussion with parents, together with their own observations during the child's first month at school, would yield a great deal of relevant information without a formal questionnaire being necessary.

The kind of information that was considered to be helpful is itemized below.

---

* Questions which a teacher can answer using her own observation of the child in the classroom.
† Factual, routine questions which could be asked formally of parents.
‡ Questions about which parents might worry if they thought that their child was being categorized or pre-judged. These questions need to be asked when parents have been reassured about their purpose.

---

† Name of child
† Date of birth
† Age of parents when child was born: Mother   Father
† Occupation of parents: Mother
                                    Father
† Position of child in family (Please tick position and indicate age and sex of siblings.)

	eldest	2nd	3rd	4th	5th	6th	7th	8th
Position								
Sex and age								

Please tick or write comments as necessary:
‡ At what age did s/he walk unaided?
‡ At what age did s/he begin to speak?
† Is English his/her first language?
† If not, what is the child's first language?
‡ At what age did s/he say words in phrases or sentences?
* Is s/he talkative now?
* Is his/her use of language advanced?
* Is there any difficulty in pronouncing certain words or sounds?
* If yes, what words or sounds?
* Can s/he dress him/herself now?
‡ At what age did s/he begin to try to dress him/herself?
* Can s/he do up zips   buttons   buckles   laces?
* Does s/he like to organize his/her playmates or be organized by them?
* Does s/he mix easily?
* Does s/he prefer to play alone?
* Does s/he prefer to play with older children?
* Does s/he prefer to do more adult activities?
‡ Does s/he have a bedtime story read to him/her regularly?
‡ If yes, at what age did this start?
‡ At what age did s/he stop having a daytime sleep?
‡ Does s/he sleep well at night?

* Is s/he a physically active child?
* Does s/he become easily bored?
† What are his/her favourite occupations?
* Is s/he very adventurous?
* Does s/he ask many questions?
* If yes, are the questions at a child's level or at an adult level? (e.g. Do you ever have to find out the answer for yourself first?)
* Can you give any examples?
* Does s/he want to know how things are made?
* Does s/he want to know how things work?
* Can s/he recognize own written name?
* Can s/he write own name?
* Is s/he right-handed   left-handed?
* Does s/he like to write and draw?
* Can s/he use scissors?
* Can s/he recognize simple words?
* Can s/he read sentences?   simple books?
‡ If yes to books, which books has s/he read?
* Has s/he a keen sense of humour?
* Can you give examples?
* Does s/he have a good memory?
* Can you give any examples?
† Has s/he been to a playgroup or nursery?
† If yes, which one?
† Does s/he look forward to coming to school?
† Is s/he apprehensive or reluctant?
† Has s/he been referred to or attended any clinics before entering school?
† If yes, which and what for?
† Is attendance continuing?
† Does s/he suffer any illness likely to cause absence from school? e.g. asthma, convulsions, eczema?
† If yes, what?
† In case of convulsions or asthma, what course of action would you like us to follow? Please state in detail.

† Is there anything else concerning your child's early development that you think we should know? e.g.
difficulties at birth
feeding problems
sleeping problems
other problems

Chapter 6

Using Objective Tests

Standardized group intelligence tests

Observations, no matter now perceptive, are highly subjective and standardized group tests can be useful to corroborate a teacher's subjective assessment that a child has a high level of reasoning ability and/or sound mastery of certain basic skills. They can also alert a teacher to a child in whom these skills had not previously been recognized and can make her observations more specific and exact. However, most tests available to teachers are the 'read: pencil and paper' type and are, therefore, limited in the type of 'intelligence' they measure. Children participating in practical problem-solving activities may manifest quite different 'intelligence'. Children who are mechanically inventive and conceptualize in three-dimensional forms are not given the opportunity to demonstrate this ability and children with poor reading skills are also disadvantaged by such tests. Moreover, standardized tests of intelligence tend to require convergent thinking and give no opportunity for a child to manifest creative or divergent thinking. The 'intelligence' measured by one test may differ significantly from the 'intelligence' measured by another and the selection of any group test requires a professional understanding of what kind of information is revealed by the particular test used. Test results must be related to the child's performance in the classroom and closely allied to the teacher's subjective understanding. Used wisely, however, they provide an objective evaluation of the child's performance on certain skills in comparison with other children of the same age group.

Selecting a group test

Firstly, the teacher should analyse *why* s/he is testing and what kind of information is required. In order to discriminate between the most able children in a group, a test should have a fairly high level of difficulty for the group as a whole. Also, a test with a reasonably high age-ceiling should be selected in preference to one with a narrow age-range. However, such a test would be unsuitable for less able pupils. The test chosen should demonstrate several aspects of a pupil's ability or several different tests should be used. The validity of the test is obviously important, i.e. whether the test actually measures what it claims to measure.

Group tests are usually classified into verbal and non-verbal categories. The verbal items include tasks such as:

selecting the appropriate word to complete a sentence or a set,
classifying words according to specified criteria,
making comparisons and contrasts using verbs and adjectives,
selecting the odd word out.

Included in the verbal category are items which test numerical skills,
for example, the four rules of number, concepts such as 'more than',
'less than', 'equal to', in the contexts of weight, size and value. These
verbal components reflect a high degree of 'learned' skills and a child
who is achieving well at school usually scores very highly on such tests.
The verbal components are also good *predictors* of school success since
most school tests and examinations require a pupil to demonstrate these
abilities.

Non-verbal items in a test require the pupil to analyse and reason
from pictures or diagrams. They include:

matching shapes,
completing a sequence of patterns,
selecting the 'odd' shape,
comparing and contrasting sets of shapes, patterns, sequences,
decoding, reversing, re-aligning, rotating.

Non-verbal tests are *less dependent* upon learned skills. They require a
child to analyse 'neutral' information, to absorb complexity of symbolic
representation and to re-order or complete patterns.

Many under-achieving pupils score highly on non-verbal tests and
much lower (by more than one standard deviation)[1] on verbal tests.
Moreover, with the strong emphasis placed by schools on verbal written
skills in language and number, there is far less opportunity for pupils
who are highly able in spatial/figural areas of mental functioning to
demonstrate their abilities. To assess a child's performance purely on a
verbal test of intelligence is to give a one-sided assessment of the child.
Thus non-verbal tests not only balance the assessment but possibly
identify under-achievers or pupils particularly able in spatial/figural
perception.

Tests should also be evaluated from a practical standpoint: cost, ease
of administration, clarity and time consumption should be assessed
against usefulness and the quality of information which is revealed
about the child.

Interpretation of tests
Interpretation of tests requires care and teachers should examine the
details of the population used for the standardization of the test. The
performance of the particular child can only be compared with that of
other children in the light of the population on which the test was
standardized.

Another important consideration is the degree of reliability of the test, i.e. whether the child's score would be consistent on repeated testing. No measurement instrument or procedure is perfect and a reliability coefficient[2] of above 0·8 would be satisfactory.

Scores may be influenced by familiarity or lack of familiarity with the type of test used. Practice or special coaching might alter an individual's score and some pupils might be lucky guessers! A child might be subject to fluctuations in attention span, memory, or motor coordination, or might be discouraged if s/he becomes confused over a particular item. In addition, a child might be physically uncomfortable in the room in which the test is taking place, or distracted by noise or interruptions. The child might have a personal worry or emotional strain, be unwell or tired.

Intelligence tests are subject to cultural bias. Bilingual children from ethnic or cultural minority groups are obvious examples of children for whom standardized test scores may not be valid. There are also more subtle but nevertheless real differences of language between social classes which may influence a child's ability to interpret the test. The following items are taken from the Black Intelligence Test of Cultural Homogeneity for the black population of New York.[3]

1 *Alley Apple* means:
   (a) Brick
   (b) Piece of fruit
   (c) Dog
   (d) Horse

2 *Black Draught* means:
   (a) Winter's cold wind
   (b) Laxative
   (c) Black soldier
   (d) Dark beer

3 *Blood* means:
   (a) A vampire
   (b) A dependent individual
   (c) An injured person
   (d) A brother of color

4 *Boogie Jugie* means:
   (a) Tired
   (b) Worthless
   (c) Old
   (d) Well put together

(*Answers* 1(a), 2(b), 3(d), 4(b))

This idiomatic language would obviously preclude a typically British child from achieving a high score and although the language difference is very obvious in this instance, the same principle of handicap applies with more subtle language or social-class differences.

The personality of the child also impinges on performance. Some children become very apprehensive in a formal test situation, particularly if they are used to an informal style of working. Others find working to a strict time limit very stressful if they are usually allowed plenty of time to think about and to finish their work. A number of children like to reflect and ponder over questions. For some very able children group tests are inadequate tests of their ability because they are thinking above the level of the test and look for difficulties where none exist. Others see alternative answers or perceive a subtle difference in meaning which is not intended. Eleven-year-old Kim paused for several minutes during a timed verbal reasoning test and said afterwards, when her teacher asked her why she had stopped for a while, 'I was just wondering about the mentality of the person who wrote that test! Some of the questions were so silly!'

Nevertheless, a high score on a group test does indicate high performance *on those particular skills* but a low result may not give a true indication of the child's potential.

The administration of group tests

The room in which the test is taken should be warm, comfortable and quiet. Preferably, it should be the one most familiar to the children. One of the weaknesses of group tests is that the teacher cannot easily observe all the children individually and, therefore, the teacher's full attention must be given throughout the test so that a child who needs help can be spotted immediately. However, the test instructions given in the manual must not be changed since they are explicitly presented so that the test is given to different groups in exactly the same way. This obviously helps to reduce the possible variables and allows comparisons between groups to be more accurately made. Hence, a pupil can only be helped within the limits laid down by the manual, and time limits must be rigidly observed.

Interpreting test scores

The result of a test is called a *raw score* which is the actual number of items scored correctly. This raw score is meaningless until applied to a *point of reference*. There are two types of points of reference: firstly, *norm referencing* which relates an individual pupil's score to the scores of other pupils; secondly, *criterion referencing* which relates the individual pupil's score to an external, independent predetermined standard. Most group tests available to teachers are norm referenced and the raw scores can be converted to standard scores, stanine scores or percentiles.

STANDARD SCORES

Most tests convert raw scores to standard scores, usually with a mean or average of 100 and a standard deviation of 15. Standard scores are based on the assumption of a normal distribution curve which is based on the distribution of test scores across a sample of the population (see Fig. 4, p. 52). Conversion of the child's raw score into a standard score makes allowances for the child's age and the teacher obtains a comparison of the performances of individual pupils of different ages. In younger age-groups in particular, wide differences in achievement exist which are primarily associated with differences in age, experience and maturity.

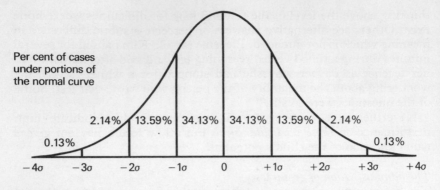

Per cent of cases
under portions of
the normal curve

2.14% 13.59% 34.13% 34.13% 13.59% 2.14%

0.13%   0.13%

-4σ -3σ -2σ -1σ 0 $+1\sigma$ $+2\sigma$ $+3\sigma$ $+4\sigma$

Standard
deviations

Fig. 4   Standard deviations

STANINE SCORES

A stanine score is based on dividing the normal distribution curve into nine divisions. The stanine score is a standard score with a mean (average) of 5 and a standard deviation of 2. Stanine scores should be regarded as representing broad bands of raw scores. They are mainly used for obtaining profiles of performance on related sets of tests.

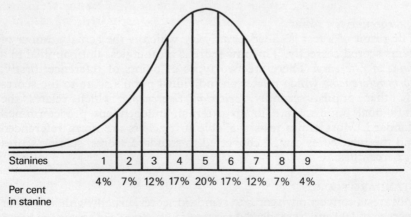

| Stanines | 1 | 2 | 3 | 4 | 5 | 6 | 7 | 8 | 9 |

4%   7%   12%   17%   20%   17%   12%   7%   4%

Per cent
in stanine

Fig. 5   Stanine scores

PERCENTILES

Percentile ranking indicates what percentage of the pupils scored lower and what percentage scored higher. A pupil at the 50th percentile has achieved a mean (average) score. The corollary is that 50 per cent would achieve a higher score. Thus the higher the percentile, the higher the pupil's ranking when compared with others of his age. A pupil scoring in the 99th percentile would indicate that only 1 per cent of the age group would score higher.

The items on standardized tests have been refined through trial and analysis. The instructions have also been formalized and finally the tests have been interpreted relative to a national population. Norm-referenced tests, regardless of their level of difficulty, compare a child's score with other children of the same age. However, cultural and educational norms change and any test results must be interpreted not only in comparison with the group but also in the light of the individual's background and experience.

CRITERION-REFERENCED TESTS

A criterion-referenced test provides information about a pupil's ability to carry out certain tasks in absolute terms and is interpreted in the light of how many items were correct regardless of group performance. If a test is measuring a pupil's ability to manipulate the concepts of weighing and measuring, for example, the necessary skills and objectives must first be outlined and the pupil's ability evaluated against the pre-determined objectives. Criterion-referenced tests are best used for specific skill testing.

In conclusion, the following list[4] summarizes the relevant questions which need to be asked in selecting group tests.

1 *Description of test items* Are the items asking for verbal, spatial, or numerical reasoning? What types of problems are being presented? What kinds of mental processes and operations are tested? What kind of intelligence is assumed?

2 *Child's task* Does the child have to read? What is the level of reading required? How does s/he need to record answers? Is much listening required? Are speed and concentration important?

3 *Format of test and method of administration* Does the test have re-usable booklets? Are there separate scoring sheets? Is there strong motivational appeal? Is the test visually attractive?

4 *Description of score* What kinds of scores are given? Standard scores, deviation quotients, percentiles? Is there one score or several? How high is the test ceiling?

5 *Description of standardized population* With whom is the child being compared? How representative is the standardization population? How many pupils were in each age group? Are all age groups covered?

6 *Validity* Do results on this test equate well with results on other measures of ability or attainment? Would you *expect* results on this test to predict performance in other areas of achievement? If so, what are they?

7 *Reliability* Does the manual give reliability data? If so, what is it? Is it adequate? What factors might adversely affect the reliability of an individual's score on any one administration of the test?

8 *Interpretation of test scores* What functional description could be given of a child who achieved a high score on this test? Briefly describe the child in terms of intellectual strengths revealed by the test.

9 *General suitability of test for identifying high ability* Comment on the appropriateness of the test for this purpose. Are there any limitations? Are there any special advantages or disadvantages?

Assessing infant school children

Group tests of intelligence are generally unsuitable for young infant school children since the relationship between group intelligence test scores obtained below 7+ years of age and later test scores is generally weak. Assessment of infant school pupils should be based largely on teacher observation of such factors as speed of learning, powers of retention, understanding of number concepts, language and expression, reading fluency and comprehension. However, a number of objective group tests can supplement the teacher's subjective assessment. A child's drawings can reveal advanced perceptual awareness: attention to detail, a sense of perspective and angle, a striving for expression and communication at a more advanced level can indicate a child of exceptional intellectual ability. The Goodenough *Draw A Man Test*[5] provides a guide to perceptual maturity and is very easily administered in the classroom. The English Picture Vocabulary Test[6] assesses listening skills and verbal comprehension independent of reading ability; and the Boehm Test of Basic Concepts[7] is designed to measure children's mastery of concepts considered necessary for achievement in the first years of school.

Reading fluency and comprehension

A high level of *reading* and *comprehension* at an early stage is usually an indication of exceptional ability. Ability to absorb and retain complex coding, to analyse, transfer and use the coding in other contexts are positive indicators of intelligence. An equal emphasis must be given to a high level of comprehension: mechanical recognition of words achieved through repetitive practice or 'barking at print' is not reading with understanding and retention. It is very common for an exceptionally able infant or junior pupil to have a reading age several years ahead of chronological age.

A very able child is often reading before s/he comes to school, but if not, s/he usually accelerates through the stages of learning to read. Difficulties may occur if the stages of reading are presented too slowly so that instead of experiencing increasing joy, the child is frustrated or bored. A reading scheme with its set stages and practice at each stage is usually inappropriate for a very able child and the teacher needs to be sufficiently skilled and confident to sidestep the usual sequential stages and select and structure appropriate reading experiences.

Very able children have an advanced level of understanding and find many infant reading books inadequate in content, style and depth. Some children have a dialogue with the print, commenting on the story as they read, and criticizing unsatisfactory outcomes or inadequate characterization.

John, at six, was reading the 'Pirate' books. There was a red pirate, who loses his hat, a green pirate, who forgets his knife, and a blue pirate who leaves his boots on the island. After reading this, John looked up with disgust and, with great exasperation, commented that it was a very stupid book because everyone knew that pirates were fierce men who sailed the seas and attacked other ships to steal treasure. They were certainly not silly men who forgot things like a hat, a knife or a pair of boots!

Mary, at six-and-a-half years, read the story of the bear who fished in a river with his tail. The bear did not notice the river was freezing until he tried to pull his tail out and found it was frozen in the ice. She wanted to know how the blood in the tail could freeze since blood was pumped around the body by the heart and would continuously pass through the tail at a constant temperature.

The development of children's reading skill needs to be assessed and monitored and the criteria for selecting a suitable reading test are similar to those for selecting group tests of intelligence. Different tests measure different kinds of reading skills.

What is required of the child?
What does the test reveal about the child's level of skill and understanding?
What *kind* of reading is being measured?
Is the test attractive, relevant and interesting?

A test such as the Neale Analysis of Reading Ability[8] is a good example of a diagnostic reading test which measures a reading age between six and 13·6 years of age. The test assesses fluency, accuracy and comprehension and the teacher systematically records the types of errors made and the reader's attitude and response.

The Edinburgh Reading Tests,[9] which indicate a reading age from seven to sixteen years also aim to assess levels of vocabulary, understanding of syntax, sequencing and comprehension. Their particular diagnostic value lies in the profiles of strengths and weaknesses of reading skills associated with successful learning and advanced study.

Although a high level of reading fluency and comprehension usually indicates a child of exceptional mental ability, there are several points which need careful attention. Many fluent readers enjoy reading aloud to the teacher and to other children and they read with expression, drama and obvious enjoyment, but some very fluent *silent* readers loathe reading aloud. They are hesitant, lack expression and *appear* to have very poor reading skills. They tend to read silently, at speed, often skimming and scanning very efficiently, and they find it difficult to read slowly and aloud to others. But their *understanding* and their ability to *retain* and *use* what they read is obvious.

Some children read avidly and so prolifically that they learn to pick out the key words and sometimes their written work is a reflection of their 'shorthand' style of reading. Their spelling is sometimes very careless. This may be because the children attempt to record very rapidly or because they read a word as a whole and do not pause long enough to see the sequence of separate letters.

Many very able children are avid readers, often to the exclusion of other hobbies and interests. Books offer them intellectual stimulus and excitement, and allow them to explore different worlds *at an appropriate level*. Science fiction, astronomy, space exploration and electronics are common interests, possibly because most books on these subjects not only supply the elementary data but also accelerate quickly into detail and depth, and a child can thus teach him/herself more easily. Moreover, these topics allow children to move from the immediate work into a broader context, and often feed their awareness of a wider world and a fascination with the themes of time, past and present; the universe; evolution and change.

Many children read advanced reference books and favourite areas are early history and natural history. Again, this may reflect their acute interest in the origins, patterns and processes of the world around them. However, many pupils have much wider interests and delve into a variety of literature and reference but all at a much more advanced level than other children.

Since the manual skills of very able pupils are usually 'normal' and run parallel with their physical development, sometimes such children conceptualize what they want to create or invent but lack the manual dexterity to transform the sophisticated idea into a satisfying artefact. Such a child is aware of the discrepancy between idea and finished product and, being very self-critical, is therefore often reluctant to engage in art or craft work. Since reading is so much more personally satisfying, it is easy to understand why these children escape into books rather than engage in more practical activities. The problem exacerbates itself since the child who is an avid reader consequently has even less practice in developing manual dexterity than most other children. In the practical workshops which form part of the primary curriculum extension courses many children produce messy paintings, or inventions that fall apart, or end up with more paint on themselves than on the paper! Teachers frequently comment that the finished product is an inadequate expression of the child's ideas or intentions.

A very able child who has a high level of reading fluency and comprehension needs both fiction and reference books which satisfy both emotional and intellectual needs. This usually means that the teacher needs to supply a reading diet quite different from that for other children (see Appendix C, p.119, for further case studies).

Individual assessment by an educational psychologist

When a teacher has assembled all available evidence about a child's background, personality, abilities and performance, and there are some inconsistencies or an obvious need for further diagnostic assessment, she should refer the child to the educational psychologist.

The test most commonly used is the Wechsler Intelligence Scale for Children (revised version), usually referred to as the WISC(R). Children from six to sixteen years can be tested, although the Wechsler Pre-School and Primary Scale of Intelligence is available for younger children. The WISC(R) has five sub-tests which provide a verbal and a non-verbal or performance score, which together provide a full scale score. (Each group has an additional sub-test which is usually omitted.)

The verbal sub-tests include:

Recall of knowledge A test of general knowledge and recall of information;
Understanding of knowledge A test of comprehension where the child is given a series of events and invited to explain certain aspects/causes;
Numerical skills Basic arithmetic skills are tested with the child being given the problems verbally;
Reasoning The child is asked to identify and reason through explanations of similarities and relationships;
Verbal ability A test of vocabulary – explaining meanings of words.

The non-verbal or performance sub-tests include:

Analysis of a complex whole A test of block design which involves analysis of a pattern and the replication of that pattern;
Analysis of parts of a whole The child has to identify the missing part in a series of pictures;
Identification of the whole from parts The child has to arrange pictures in logical sequence;
Synthesis of the whole from parts Jigsaw pieces are arranged to make a whole;
Sequencing symbols and digits Codes, numbers and symbols are arranged in order.

The test takes about an hour to administer and the psychologist, after establishing rapport with the child, is able to observe carefully and to interpret not only the child's test scores but also his/her reactions to the test, style of working etc.

Following this individual assessment, the psychologist is able to discuss the needs of the child with both parents and teachers, providing guidance and support where necessary.

In discussion of the strategies outlined in Chapters 3–6 which may be used to identify very able children, I have stressed the importance of both subjective and objective methods of assessment, although the intuitive, sensitive awareness of a creative teacher is of first importance. On the basis of such assessment, the teacher can diagnose the child's strengths and weaknesses and the level of current attainment so that appropriate learning experiences can be provided.

Although assessment of a pupil's abilities should be a continuous process, the most important phase of a child's school life is, perhaps, the infant school, when feelings of success or failure, joy or unhappiness, frustration or satisfaction, provide the first experiences of school-based education. Hence I have stressed the importance of the early identification of very able pupils before possible problems become deep and intractable and behaviour patterns arising from frustration or under-achievement mask a pupil's true potential.

References

[1] The standard deviation is a measure of the dispersion of the scores from the average score. Fig. 5 on p. 52 shows normalized distribution.

[2] Reliability coefficient is a measure of the correlation between two forms of a test, between scores on two administrations of the same test or between two halves of a test.

[3] WILLIAMS, R. L. 'The Black Intelligence Test of Cultural Homogeneity' in TUCKMAN, B. W. (1975) *Measuring Educational Outcomes* New York: Harcourt Brace Jovanovich Inc.

[4] WALLACE, B. and ACKLAW, J. (1981) *Identifying Bright Pupils: A Teacher's Guide and Handbook*. Essex Education Authority

[5] GOODENOUGH *Draw A Man Test* Slough: NFER

[6] BRIMER, S. and DUNN, J. (1962) *The British Picture Vocabulary Scale* London: NFER/Nelson

[7] BOEHM, A. (1970) *Boehm Test of Basic Concepts* New York: Psychological Corporation

[8] *Neale Analysis of Reading Ability* London: Macmillan

[9] *The Edinburgh Reading Tests* (1977) London: Hodder and Stoughton

PART TWO
Providing for Very Able Pupils

Chapter 7

Curriculum Development

Unless the idea of a special school or class for very able children is accepted, the classroom teacher will need to cope with such pupils in the classroom for most of the time. Before she can begin to do this, there must be a personal commitment to and a professional understanding and acceptance of *the need to provide differentiated individual and group assignments in the classroom.*

The basic principle of designing individualized learning is to provide a background of materials and experiences to which each pupil can respond at a level appropriate for him/her. The fundamental task of the teacher is to select appropriate learning experiences in consultation with the pupil: it is a process of negotiation, a synthesis of the teacher's breadth of professional understanding, knowledge of the subject and its divergent opportunities, and the child's interests, skills and level of understanding.

To make appropriate curriculum decisions the teacher needs to know both the progressive stages of the relevant educational objectives and also the sets of concepts encompassed in the specific curriculum areas. Extension programmes must be logical outgrowths, not merely random involvement in whatever happens to be available.

The specific difference in planning curriculum activities for very able children lies not in the *approach* but in the *pace* and the *depth* of the learning experiences presented. The pace and depth are largely dependent upon:

the quality of the teacher's questioning;
the quality and complexity of the pupil's activity;
the removal of unnecessary repetitive practice;
the availability of adequate resources.

In considering both the quality of the teacher's questioning and the level of the pupil's activity and response, it is necessary to have some guidelines against which to examine them. Teachers need a framework within which to work and from which to diverge and Bloom's taxonomies of the cognitive and affective domains[1] provide convenient initial guides. This, obviously, is not the only possible framework but Bloom succinctly provides a checklist against which curriculum content can be judged for its value, balance and intellectual demand. The checklist can be used as the springboard for the teacher to analyse why s/he is promoting and encouraging certain activities. Although such a checklist may artificially differentiate and isolate aspects of thinking and learning, it helps the teacher to refine her thinking before integrating and combining elements into a whole.

Dr Trevor Kerry's research into teacher's questioning skills points very clearly to the need for such a framework against which teachers can evaluate not only the level of their own functioning but also that of their pupils.[2] Kerry examined the questioning skills of 36 teachers in first-year secondary mixed-ability classes. His overall findings were, after analysing a total of 6,928 questions, that:

21 per cent of the questions were concerned with classroom management;

75·5 per cent were concerned with informing and checking that information has been received;

3·5 per cent were concerned with exploration at the higher cognitive levels.

While it is important for pupils to acquire knowledge, the dearth of questions to promote higher-order levels of cognitive thinking indicates cause for concern, particularly since very able pupils *need* to function at these higher levels if their learning experiences are to be fulfilling and personally satisfying. Although Kerry's analysis of teacher questioning took place in first-year comprehensive classes, his findings point to the need to examine the quality of teacher questioning in all classes with pupils of all ages.

Bloom's taxonomy

It would now seem appropriate to discuss Bloom's taxonomy in detail, and explore what is meant by the higher-order thinking skills. Once these principles are understood, they can be applied in the planning process of the curriculum extension project (see Chapter 8, pp. 73ff.).

A summary of cognitive abilities based on Bloom's taxonomy
1 KNOWLEDGE
The acquisition of various forms of knowledge is learning at its most basic level, although this first level is the springboard for other forms of learning. Children cannot learn in a vacuum, they must have content before they can begin to use and act upon it. They must have information and data about which they can think; they need the knowledge of relevant techniques and mastery of appropriate skills. Acquiring knowledge involves memory, repetition and description and includes knowledge of appropriate materials, methods, processes, patterns and structures: e.g.

specific terminology and symbols (e.g. terms and symbols used in map reading or mathematics);

appropriate methodology and techniques (e.g. methods of ecological study or various techniques in art or craft);

relevant facts and theories (e.g. established historical fact and the theories of causation, accepted scientific data and the associated theory, or knowledge of literature);

ways of studying, organizing and judging;

ways of presenting materials, styles and usual formats;

accepted classifications, trends, sequences and categories.

The acquiring of knowledge in the context outlined above involves the pupil in receiving what is considered the best or the essential core of the culture's established body of knowledge. Very able pupils can acquire such knowledge extremely rapidly and retain it. They need, therefore, to be presented with knowledge in depth and without a great deal of repetition. Very often they have no need to make extensive (or sometimes any) notes at all, and can debate issues or apply the knowledge acquired immediately. Many very able pupils complain that they 'rewrite textbooks'. Also, although certain kinds of knowledge are essential to further learning, one of the most important requisites for independent learning is knowing where to find the required information which will provide the basis for action.

2 COMPREHENSION

The pupil is required to demonstrate in the following ways some understanding of the knowledge acquired:

Translation is the most basic level of comprehension and includes: paraphrasing, explaining the meaning of words and selecting relevant information to answer a question.

Interpretation demands a higher level of comprehension and includes: taking facts and re-ordering them, presenting a new view of the material, comparing and contrasting, and grouping or classifying according to specified criteria.

Extrapolation elicits the highest level of comprehension and asks the pupil to use given data to determine consequences and effects; to ascertain causes, implications, corollaries and results.

Teachers generally concentrate on the acquiring of knowledge and the first level of comprehension, i.e. translation. The higher levels of comprehension, however, together with the next four categories of application, analysis, synthesis and evaluation, constitute the higher-order thinking skills. Although all children should gradually be led into functioning, as far as they are able, within these higher-order thinking skills, the very characteristic which identifies exceptionally able children is their ability to use the higher-order thinking skills with ease and in depth at an earlier age than other children.

3 APPLICATION
Knowledge is static and passive unless it is applied to *solving* problems. Application should involve:

  using acquired knowledge in different areas of study and in the light of new content;
  applying acquired practices and theories to solving problems;
  transferring methods or techniques to new situations;
  bringing general principles to bear upon new questions.

Again, while all children should apply their knowledge to problem-solving, very able children can tackle more complex and demanding tasks. The whole purpose of education is to develop understanding of the child's immediate and wider world and to prepare him/her to anticipate and cope with situations and problems which may arise. In a time of rapid change and uncertainty, education should be promoting flexible thinking and adaptability in new situations.

4 ANALYSIS
Analysis involves the process of breaking down the whole to clarify the relationship between the constituent parts. The activity involves:

  differentiating between fact and hypothesis;
  identifying hidden meanings;
  finding themes or patterns;
  understanding the system or the organization.

Very able children can usually see the relationships with the minimum of help. They can see the new patterns, they are aware of the whole system and how each section or unit contributes to the whole.

5 SYNTHESIS OR CREATIVE THINKING
Synthesis is the process of creating or recombining elements to form a new whole, rearranging or reclassifying to make a new pattern or structure. Activities include:

  organizing a set of ideas to make a new statement;
  developing plans to test a new hypothesis;
  creating a new form of classifying data or phenomena;
  discovering new relationships;
  inventing and proposing alternatives;
  changing and improving.

To promote creative thinking is, of course, relevant for all children and this, possibly, is most closely linked with the personality of the teacher. Her own creative style of teaching will greatly influence the pupil's approach to their learning. Having already emphasized the importance of the teacher's questioning style, the fostering of creative thinking in particular requires a supportive, psychologically non-threatening atmosphere in which pupils can explore new pathways and unusual ideas.

6 EVALUATION

Evaluation is the process of appraising, assessing or criticizing on the basis of specific standards and criteria. Evaluation demands:

> judging on the basis of logical accuracy and consistency in argument;
> verifying the worth of evidence or proof;
> evaluating materials according to specified criteria;
> comparing and discriminating between theories and generalizations;
> assessing work against recognized excellence;
> recognizing logical fallacies;
> arbitrating in controversial or opposing arguments.

Truly evaluative thinking is, perhaps, the highest level of thinking since it involves personal decision-making based on reasoned and logical argument supported by valid evidence. A major criticism often levelled at the education that takes place in schools is that children are fed ideas and are presented with conclusions which they tend to accept without critical appraisal of their validity or worth. Often children are not encouraged to check the evidence on which an historian or scientist, for example, bases his/her work. Published text is assumed to be correct and hence the ideas expressed therein are 'right' ideas.

How can pupils develop into thinking, questioning adults if teachers do not encourage questioning skills? Far too often, a quiet classroom in which children are writing industriously is seen as a 'good class' and the teacher as a 'good teacher and disciplinarian'. While there are times, certainly, when children need the opportunity and the right atmosphere to think and write reflectively, they also need to *talk*, to *debate* and to *explore ideas* with the teacher and with one another. It is, sadly, very common that when groups of exceptionally able children are brought together for particular courses, they have to be provoked or sometimes goaded into asking questions, querying assumptions and the validity of evidence. Many are too used to receiving from the teacher or the book, memorizing and then repeating what has been learned. It is exhilarating, though, to see how quickly they begin to question critically once they realize such questioning is not only acceptable but expected. Some pupils, however, feel threatened by the open exploration of ideas. They have been used to automatic, safe and often unthinking response and need reassurance that intellectual exploration is a worthy adventure. Of course, all children need to be encouraged to ask questions but since many very able children will become leaders in various fields, fostering their questioning skills is particularly essential.

This analysis of activities which should be incorporated into curriculum extension projects applies to the cognitive domain. Before applying those principles in practice, we need to redress the balance of emphasis. Implicit and often explicit in what has been said has been the importance of the child growing and maturing as a social being in a climate of psychological security, and a teacher should examine the learning which a child needs to cope with this aspect of personal development. Again, a summary of Bloom's ideas forms a useful checklist.

A summary of the affective domain based on Bloom's taxonomy
1 RECEIVING
  developing personal awareness: building a consciousness of situations, phenomena, objects, stages of affairs, through the senses;
  perceptions of colour, arrangement, form, design;
  awareness of the symbolic representation of things, people, situations.
Receiving from others
  listening to others;
  appreciating and tolerating religious, political, social and national differences;
  developing sensitivity to human needs and social problems.
Selected/specific awareness
  listening and discriminating between moods and meanings, for example, in music;
  perceiving differences in human values and judgments through media such as literature.

2 RESPONDING
  accepting basic rules for order and safety;
  participating voluntarily in activities;
  accepting personal responsibilities;
  seeking and deriving personal satisfaction through tasks pursued and accomplished;
  seeking and responding with pleasure to forms of self-expression and personal enrichment.

3 VALUING AND APPRECIATING WORTH
  internalizing social values and developing personal values;
  ascribing worth to a phenomenon, behaviour, object;
  commitment to a value (e.g. honesty, fair play);
  discriminating between values (e.g. liberty and licence);
  pursuing a faith, a loyalty, an ideal (e.g. religious or political ideas);
  assuming responsibility for social action (e.g. holding a meeting or signing a petition);
  commitment to action motivated by personal convictions (e.g. fighting for democracy or human rights).

4 ORGANIZATION FOR LIVING AND PERSONAL PHILOSOPHY
conceptualizing a value, identifying abstract qualities (e.g. worth/beauty);
relating abstract qualities to life (e.g. anti-pollution or the Welfare State);
organizing and ordering complex and disparate values (e.g. appreciating the interests of the minority v. the majority);
synthesizing a new value (e.g. discussing the consequences of a new invention);
developing a consistent system of values (e.g. planning a new town);
willingness to revise judgments in terms of issues, purposes, consequences (e.g. altering plans or proposed actions in the light of experience or new evidence).

An analysis of psychomotor domain

Finally we come to the psychomotor domain. Teachers of young children necessarily tend to be more aware of needs in this area than their secondary colleagues; but a glance at the list will show that these are areas of skill that are required, and developed, well into adult life.

1 PHYSICAL DEVELOPMENT
simple reflex movements, perceptual abilities, simple and complex movements.

2 GROWTH PROBLEMS
recognizing and accepting motor-development abilities;
accepting divergences in physical development;
recognizing and accepting sex role.

3 MOTOR DEVELOPMENT
experimenting, manipulating and exploring to gratify intellectual curiosity.

4 SKILLED MOVEMENT
writing, developing skilled techniques, using machinery, tools;
involvement in sport, dance, music.

5 STRUCTURE AND HEALTHY FUNCTIONING OF THE HUMAN BODY
physical and chemical;
mental and psychological.

6 TOTAL MOVEMENT AS A PERONS
individual personality and group dynamics: understanding the self and the group;
using and responding to non-verbal communication, developing sensitivity and awareness to other people's needs.

What has been said in this chapter encapsulates these messages:

1   All children, including the very able, should be educated according to their individual capacities.
2   In order to do this, teachers need to adopt an individualized teaching approach.
3   This individualized approach implies the need to develop curriculum materials in a systematic and planned way.
4   Very able pupils not only need to accelerate through basic stages to depth but also to be given opportunity to use the higher-order thinking skills.

In Chapter 8 we will go on to look in more detail at ways to plan and execute a curriculum for the very able.

References

[1]BLOOM, B.S. (1965) *Taxonomy of Educational Objectives* London: Longman

[2]Dr Kerry's 1981 research involved coding questions, based on the level of *cognitive* demand. The coding system was adapted from Bloom's taxonomy, with an additional category of 'management questions'. The complete coding system was as follows:

Q0   management questions, e.g. will you sit down?
Q1   recall questions, e.g. what happened when . . . ?
Q2   simple comprehension questions, e.g. what did we say a 'col' was?
Q3   application questions, e.g. how would you find out if . . . ?
Q4   analysis questions, e.g. how does he achieve this effect?
Q5   synthesis questions, e.g. how could you rewrite this story to say . . . ?
Q6   evaluation questions, e.g. what is the evidence for . . . ?

This system of coding obviously does not include questioning within the affective domain which is concerned with social relationships or social control. The questioning strategies outlined in Kerry's groupings can be further classified into two sections: Q0, Q1 and Q2 fall into the lower-order questions and Q3, Q4, Q5, Q6 fall into the higher-order questions.

Chapter 8

Preparing Curriculum Extension Projects

The difference in planning curriculum extension projects for very able children lies in making provision for the pace and depth at which such children work. Such planning demands considerable time, and it would therefore seem not only necessary but sensible for teachers to share the preparation and pool their expertise and ideas.

Cooperative preparation

One example of cooperative preparation has been developed in Essex, where groups of teachers have undertaken to prepare curriculum project schemes at infant, junior and secondary levels.[1] Such schemes are not meant to be prescriptive: they offer suggestions for activities and provide resources which a teacher can use flexibly in negotiation with the child. The method of preparing curriculum extension projects is fully described below and is presented as one practical way to begin to meet the needs of very able pupils.

Teachers who are experienced, creative and dedicated (and there are very many of these) need to be given opportunities to pool their ideas and experiences. Such collaboration merely requires organization and time. A five-day residential course where teachers work together as a 'think tank', can yield a wealth of ideas, suggestions for activities, details of resources, references, etc.

The ideas developed by the teacher or group of teachers form a basic network of possible avenues of exploration which a child or group of children might pursue. When the teacher has prepared in this way she can then stand back, as it were, and promote discussion by asking:

What questions can we ask about this?
What aspects would it be interesting to explore?
How can we use this information or knowledge?

She can then build a project web with the pupils, suggesting some ideas to expand and complement theirs, leading them into new areas of awareness and avenues of exploration. She may well have foreseen many of the ideas they suggest and so will have researched possibilities, resources, reference books etc., so that the children can begin to develop their ideas straight away. Any new ideas which have not been anticipated can also be followed up, but it can take time to locate resources and children need to be able to follow through their ideas promptly while their enthusiasm is high. Nevertheless, children can be involved in the search for resources. Even infant pupils can write letters and will eagerly await the replies. Older pupils can *completely* structure a project, using the same process as the teachers did in their collaborative planning, but again this takes time and a teacher must carefully judge the balance between how much information the pupils can find for themselves, and how much she will provide. The art lies in anticipating possibilities and providing sufficient resources to launch the project and keep the momentum going, while allowing the pupils to search and wait for additional sources of information. Nothing destroys children's interest and enthusiasm more than having to delay work because there are no reference books or suitable materials to hand.

The process of building and negotiating a project web needs to be carried through with every group of pupils. It is gathering the resources which usually devours time, and the teachers' collaborative preparation alleviates that problem. Thus, a collection of ideas for exploration, plus possible questions and activities, together with appropriate resources provides a basis from which pupils and teachers can adventure further.

A broad curriculum model on which to base the preparation of projects has *evolved* through discussion in teacher workshops, with teachers openly exploring their needs as classroom practitioners, discussing the aims and objectives of education, and recognizing the specific needs of very able pupils. It is essential that teachers are fully involved in curriculum development, that they perceive the *need* for such development, understand the processes involved and are given the responsibility for initiating, monitoring and evaluating any innovation and development. When we talk of education developing from the needs, interests and abilities of the pupils, we should also talk about curriculum change emanating from the needs, interests and abilities of the teachers.

Most projects have been devised initially for trial on curriculum extension courses in which groups of very able children are brought together for one or several days. Such courses are valuable for several reasons. Firstly, teachers can gain first-hand experience of working with very able children, seeing their response to challenges, observing their learning styles, gaining insight into the speed and depth of work which such pupils can undertake. In the light of this experience teachers' expectations of what all children can do are raised. Without exception, teachers, after working with a group of very able children, have expressed their astonishment at the high level of the children's thinking and at the phenomenal pace of their work. Perhaps the greatest and most satisfying experience has been seeing the response of very able children from poor and deprived homes, watching under-achieving children becoming interested and motivated, or witnessing aggressive children working cooperatively. Teachers have said that they needed that insight to reassess their educational goals and lift their own understanding and expectations. Such an experience undoubtedly carries over into the classroom, despite the pressures and demands of everyday teaching which can so easily blunt ideas and atrophy vision. Many teachers have expressed feelings of deep personal intellectual satisfaction after working on a curriculum extension course since obviously many highly creative teachers experience the deadening effect of the slow pace of learning needed by some children. Teachers also need stimulus and challenge to regain an excitement in *teaching* and to persevere with the repetitive tasks and chores of school routine.

Secondly, having prepared curriculum extension activities, the teachers can evaluate their work in the light of the *pupils'* response and evaluation. Even very young pupils are capable of evaluating the quality and relevance of the activities in which they participate. Perhaps it would be a good practice to encourage *all* children to evaluate the quality of their educational experiences. It is rare to find a teacher who asks her pupils if they found the lesson interesting!

Thirdly, the projects can then be revised, refined and made available to all teachers for use in schools. Even at this stage the projects are regarded as still evolving and open to change. Each teacher who uses a project is invited to add additional ideas or to refine the ideas already presented.

Finally, the teachers who have prepared the projects have not only gained greater experience and personal insight into the needs of very able children, but they themselves have become valuable resources. Other teachers can contact them to discuss a particular project, they can take leadership roles within their own schools, and can lead further workshops with other teachers.

The three levels of planning

In the preparation of curriculum extension projects, three stages of planning are necessary:

1 Teachers collectively need to generate ideas, construct a 'possibilities plan' and decide on the curriculum areas to be explored.
2 Teachers discuss the concepts to be developed, the skills to be acquired, and the processes and the activities through which the children will learn.
3 Available resources need to be listed.

First level planning

First level planning (see Fig. 6, p. 71) looks at factors which need to be considered in the preliminary stages of planning curriculum extension

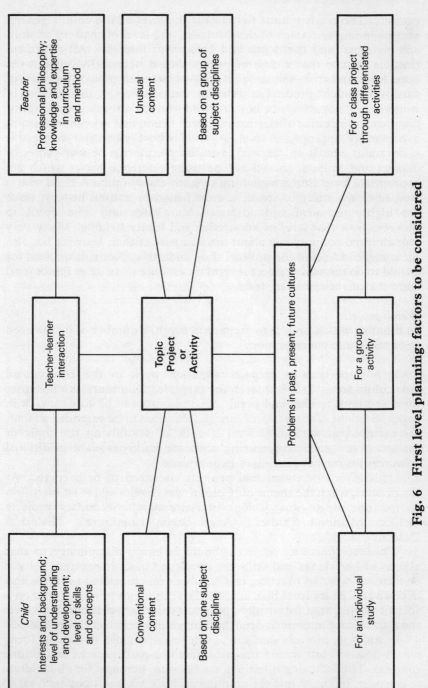

Fig. 6 First level planning: factors to be considered

projects. The teacher must first assess the level of the child's general understanding and stage of development, the level of mastery of skills and concepts, and the depth and breadth of interests. All too often, teachers assume that a class of pupils should necessarily *begin* at the same level, and from the same starting-point, even though they accept that pupils might proceed at different rates. However, this method of working may not always be best. A child who has a reading age three or four years in advance of classmates, needs fiction and reference books at a personally appropriate level. A child whose particular interest is history and who is an 'expert' in military uniforms or war-games or Tudors and Stuarts, should not be using reference books which are appropriate for children beginning to study those topics. A child who is steeped in the study of space, science fiction or natural history, often has highly technical and advanced knowledge and s/he needs to progress *from that level* of knowledge and understanding. Many very able children not only talk about the *slow pace* of their learning but also the *superficial level* of the projects they undertake. Nor is it unusual for a child to do the same project several times, once or twice at junior level and yet again at secondary level.

Which project?
In deciding which project to prepare in depth, a number of points need to be taken into consideration.

1   It is important to prepare extension work in the *conventional* curriculum areas. At infant level, for example, 'Dinosaurs' is a favourite topic and both teacher and pupils need resources to be able to work in depth. Sections of the *accepted core syllabus* need to be extended so that, for example, at secondary level if a child is studying the topic of 'pollution' or 'genetic engineering' there are readily available additional resources for further reading or experiments.
2   Unusual or unconventional projects also need to be prepared. At junior level, when the theme of 'Colour' was developed for an extension course, one aspect was 'Colour in Astronomy'. Secondary projects include 'Medieval Studies', 'Anglo-Saxon Literature', 'Historical Detective Work'.
3   Whenever possible, projects should be multi-disciplinary so that aspects of knowledge and skills are developed in an integrated, holistic or thematic way. In practice, this has been much easier to initiate and develop at primary level than at secondary, although projects based on a specific subject area are equally important since very able children often show an intense interest in detail and depth in a relatively narrow field.
4   In addition, projects should try, whenever possible, to develop ideas not in isolation but within the continuum of past, present and future contexts. The following questions are relevant, perhaps, for all children to consider, but very able children particularly ask questions such as:

What has caused this to happen?
Why is life as it is today?
What is likely to happen in the future and why?

They are very aware of global problems and complexities; they are capable of understanding the deeper significance, the more abstract generalizations, the far-reaching consequences.

5   Projects can be prepared either as class projects or group/individual projects. If they are prepared as class projects, then activities must be carefully differentiated to provide for a wide range of abilities. If group/individual projects are prepared, it can be assumed that the pupils have advanced levels of reading and understanding, can cope with complex information and have high levels of reasoning ability.

By general consensus, teachers have tended to prepare group/individual projects. They expressed the need for resources prepared at an advanced level, since they felt quite competent in preparing work for average and below average pupils and were also more familiar with resources which are currently available for pupils in these broad categories.

In the initial preparatory stages, teachers work collectively, brainstorming, and helping to develop and clarify their own and other people's ideas. Teachers also reveal their personal strengths and interests and a general topic flow-chart is generated. Fig. 7, p. 74, is an example of the first level planning of a project for exceptionally able junior pupils aged from eight to ten years.

Second level planning
Fig. 8, p. 75 summarizes the second stage or second level of planning in the preparation of curriculum extension projects. After the initial collection of ideas, each idea is extended through an analysis of the aims and objectives, skills and techniques to be incorporated. It is also necessary to have a clear understanding of the key concepts and the hierarchy of concepts to be developed with an emphasis on the *process* of learning rather than the *product*. It is at this stage that an understanding of Bloom's taxonomy (outlined in Chapter 7) enables teachers to analyse the quality of the learning experiences they are planning for the children. Pupils need to be taught how to become more efficient and independent in their learning, how and where to find the information they need, and how to organize their study. Various methods of recording and presenting work should be encouraged so that pupils do not think that 'writing it down' is necessarily the best way to record their work.

Putting principles into practice
When teachers read books about education they often exhibit a healthy

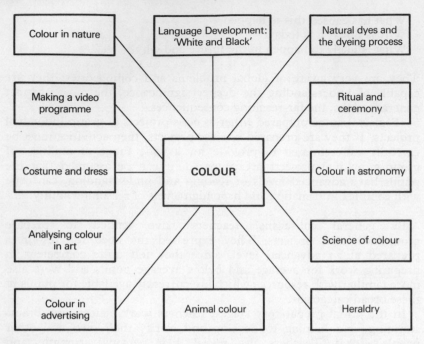

Fig. 7 'Colour': an example of first level planning

scepticism about the validity and practicality of the ideas presented. They tend to be suspicious of authors who are not practising, full-time classroom teachers. However, all the ideas presented here have been devised by teachers – initially for curriculum extension courses but subsequently all projects have been tried out in the normal classroom.

If we return to the initial flow-chart on 'Colour' (Fig. 7) which summarizes the first level planning, we can apply the principles of the second level planning outlined above to some of the sub-sections. Each project has been designed and used with very able pupils of eight to ten years of age. Obviously, not all the possible ideas for developing each sub-section can be given, but this example will demonstrate some of the questioning which might be used to encourage the higher-order thinking skills outlined on pp. 61ff. Too often, project work means that a child is merely reproducing a précis of a reference or textbook rather than responding to the text as a stimulus for thinking and action.

Taking an idea, for example 'Natural dyes and Dyeing' from the first flow-chart, the teacher (or teachers) suggest as many questions as possible from which activities can be developed (see Fig. 9, p. 76).

(I would like to acknowledge the work of Eleanor Williams in the development of the project based on 'Dyes and Dyeing'.)

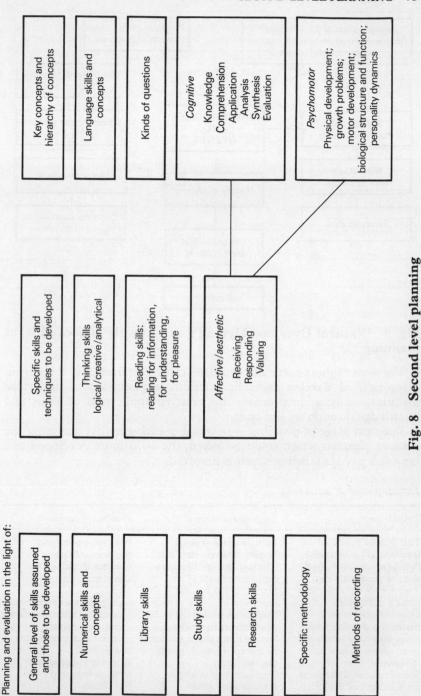

Fig. 8 Second level planning

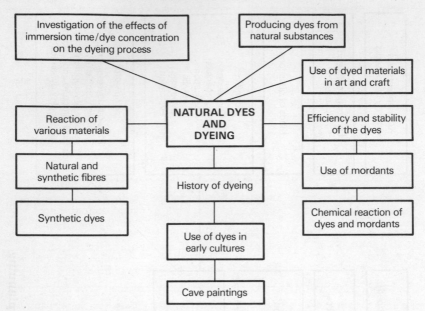

Fig. 9   'Natural Dyes and Dyeing': an example of second level planning

The aims of these particular activities can be grouped into three main categories: to develop skills in scientific exploration; to undertake historical analysis; to promote the creative application of skills and knowledge through art and craft.

The next stage of planning is to develop each activity, analysing the *kinds of questions* which could be asked, the *skills* to be developed and the *quality of the thinking* which is involved.

Development of activities

Possible questions	Suggested activities	Analysis of activities
Can dyes be produced from natural substances? What factors could affect the dye produced? e.g. does the *time* of collecting make a difference? Does it matter if the material is dried or fresh? Does the soil in which the plant grows make a difference? Does it matter if the plant grew in light or shade?	Select various fruits, berries, flowers, etc. Through group discussion, explore methods of extracting the natural pigments. Establish a sequential and efficient way of working. Decide how results should be recorded (chart, graph, diagram, etc.) Organize results into an appropriate format.	Problem-posing and problem-solving Creative thinking Developing scientific method, i.e. – suggesting an hypothesis – designing an experiment – analysing results – drawing and evaluating conclusions. Acquiring appropriate methodology and techniques.

Possible questions	Suggested activities	Analysis of activities
		Devising ways of organizing and presenting information. Using acquired knowledge to elaborate hypotheses. Classification of information according to specified criteria. Comparing and contrasting to make reasoned judgment.
What effect does – temperature – immersion time – dye concentration have on the dyeing process and finishing time?	Design experiments to examine factors which influence the process and product of dyeing.	Selection of appropriate materials for further experiments. Refinement of techniques acquired through evaluation and extension of experiments.
How fast is the dye? How stable is the colour? How do mordants work?	Find out about the use of mordants. Design experiments to examine the use and effect of mordants. Extend presentation of results. Find out about the chemical reactions of mordants. Present findings in diagramatic or any other visual form.	Acquiring knowledge of relevant facts. Research using selected references. Development of library skills, finding information, using contents and indexes, making essential notes. Designing further experiments and testing. Further research and analysis of process. Creating new and exciting ways of presenting knowledge and ideas.
How important/influential have dyes been in other cultures? For what purposes have dyes been used?	Find out about the development and use of dyes. Present information in an interesting way, e.g. an illustrated talk, preparation of an interest corner for other children. Drama presentation.	Analysis of information. Classification of the values of other cultures. Comparing and contrasting other cultures. Discriminating between values. Evaluation of the ideas and customs of other cultures. Drawing general conclusions. Sharing new knowledge with others.

Possible questions	Suggested activities	Analysis of activities
What can you make using your dyed materials?	Design and make an artefact using the dyed materials and exploring other techniques, e.g. wax resist, tie and dye, silk screening.	Using acquired knowledge and techniques to create something new.

The section on Heraldry could be developed as shown in Fig.10, p. 80.

(I would like to acknowledge the work of Mary Lewis in the development of the project based on 'Heraldry'.)

These ideas can be broadly grouped into: promoting analysis of present-day and historical symbols, studying language derivation, understanding an aspect of medieval life, and creative application of the knowledge acquired.

Elaboration of activities

Possible questions	Suggested activities	Analysis of activities
What modern signs or symbols are in common use today? Why are they necessary? How useful are they?	Collect examples of emblems/signs in everyday use. Find out about and discuss their uses and meanings. Devise various ways of sorting and grouping them and explain the reasons for such grouping. Invent a new set of signs and symbols.	Detailed observation of an aspect of our present culture. Research in order to explain meanings with justification of the reasoning. Analysis of relationships. Classification according to selected criteria. Evaluation in the light of reasoned argument. Creative thinking.
What are heraldic emblems? How and why did they develop? To what extent are they important today?	Discuss when and why heraldic signs began. Devise a way of presenting the information to other people in a clear and systematic way.	Researching to find information. Development of library skills: selecting suitable reference books, using contents and indexes. Development of note-taking skills. Classifying and presenting the information systematically. Sharing the knowledge acquired. Understanding the pattern or system.

Possible questions	Suggested activities	Analysis of activities
Can you identify the language of heraldic terms? Can you explain why a particular language(s) was commonly used? Are any of the words used in everyday language today?	Invent a way of helping you and your friends to learn the new language of heraldry, e.g. quizzes, crosswords, charts, games, flash-cards, jigsaws. Use etymological dictionaries to trace the derivation of heraldic terms. Devise ways of grouping the terms according to similarities. Invent new heraldic terms to suit the space age.	Creation of interesting and challenging ways to master the new terminology of heraldry. Analysis and deduction of meaning and structure. Classification. Analysis of relationships and the finding of patterns and themes. Creative thinking.
Can you find any heraldic signs in your neighbourhood? Why are they used and what do they mean?	Explore your neighbourhood to find heraldic signs. Plan an exciting trail for a visitor, making up clues and an interesting guidebook.	Observation of the environment, development of interest in and understanding of own culture; an awareness of the symbolic representation of things. Creation of something new to share with others.
What characteristics identify you and your family – past history, occupations, hobbies?	Design and make a personal coat of arms. Invent symbols to represent characteristics of your family or use symbols you have already learned about. Find out the derivation of family, street, district names. Discuss the significance of, and invent, a family motto.	Ordering and discriminating between personal and community values. Designing a new system. Research using library skills. Use of knowledge in a different context. Valuing human motives and ascribing worth to personal and social ideals.
Imagine you are a medieval knight; what vows and promises would you consider important? What vows or promises would you be willing to make and why?	Debate the importance of the knight's training and vows. Design a medieval scroll and write some personal promises or vows on it. Find out if other people would make similar vows.	Research to find out the details of the knight's training and vows. Valuing the worth of ideals and loyalties. Discriminating between ideals and loyalties and making personal decisions based on reasoned argument. Comparing personal values with other people's to develop awareness and understanding.

Possible questions	Suggested activities	Analysis of activities
What can you deduce about medieval life through the study of historical paintings?	Study a selection of medieval pictures of knights, tournaments and crusades (e.g. the Bayeux Tapestry). Discuss the historical value of these.	Use of available evidence to make hypotheses and deductions.

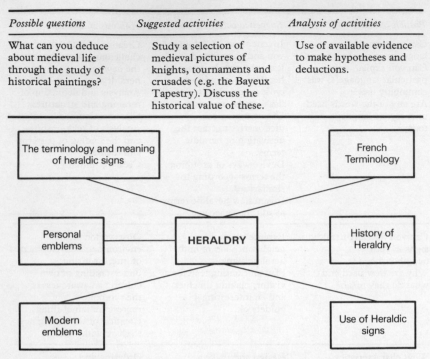

Fig. 10 'Heraldry': an example of second level planning

Another section – Language Development: 'White and Black' – could be developed as shown in Fig. 11, below.

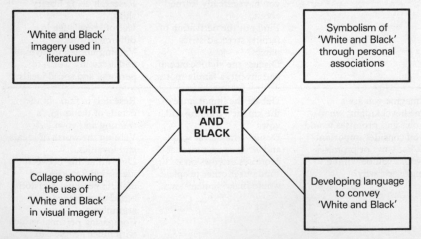

Fig. 11 'Language Development: White and Black': an example of second level planning

(I would like to acknowledge the work of Marilyn Lampey in the development of the project based on 'Language Development: White and Black'.)

The aim of this project is to develop creative writing through an understanding of the symbolism of 'White and Black'. Pupils explore and evaluate aspects of literature, examining the potential power of imagery and discussing their own and other people's responses. They are encouraged to use language both definitively and creatively, to analyse and refine ideas.

Elaboration of activities

Possible questions	Suggested activities	Analysis of activities
What ideas and feelings are conveyed to you by the word 'white'?	Brainstorm ideas and feelings associated with 'white'. Discuss common ideas and feelings and individual ideas and feelings. Explore reasons for different and unusual ideas.	Creative exploration of ideas. Analysis of relationships. Classification of ideas according to specified criteria. Comparing and contrasting. Looking at personal and group values.
What ideas and feelings are conveyed by these pictures? How do you think this is achieved?	Collect pictures which use the image of 'white'. See how many ways you can sort the pictures into groups. Explain your reasons for your groupings. Make a collage(s) of the pictures you have collected to illustrate your groupings.	Detailed observation of an aspect of the culture. Further analysis of relationships with classification of meanings, themes. Presentation of the thinking task using a visual format.
What words and phrases are important to you in conveying the image of 'white'?	Collect words and phrases associated with 'white'. Assemble the words in a stylized poem.* Make up a new pattern and assemble words to convey exciting images, ideas and feelings.	Creative exploration of words and phrases. Refinement of ideas and the use of language.

Possible questions	Suggested activities	Analysis of activities
How do other poets and writers use language to convey images, ideas and feelings associated with 'white'?	Read a selection of poems and stories. Choose words, phrases and short passages which convey 'white' or associations of 'white' to you. Tape-record your choice of literature; discuss the reasons for your choice. Choose appropriate music to accompany your choice of literature. Collect some prints of famous paintings which convey the image of 'white'.	Research in literature. Creative exploration of ideas. Critical analysis of writer's ideas and imagery. Creative exploration of music and paintings.

*In this instance, the stylized poem was deliberately structured as follows:

Making diamond poems

$$\text{White}$$

$$\text{X} \quad \text{White} \quad \text{X}$$

$$\text{X} \quad \text{X} \quad \text{White} \quad \text{X} \quad \text{X}$$

$$\text{X} \quad \text{White} \quad \text{X}$$

$$\text{White}$$

The poem is five lines long. The middle of the poem is a column of 'white', written five times. The first and last line consist of the word 'white' only. The second and fourth lines need two more words, one either side of the central 'white'. The middle line requires two words either side of 'white'.

The advantage of this exercise is that it allows for a great deal of thinking and revising without a bulk of words that would be too tedious to cope with. It also illuminates, very clearly, the crucial importance of every word; with only eight words, one word out of place mars the whole.

Marilyn Lampey, who developed this aspect of the project, wanted to encourage creative writing within a set structure, in order to focus the children's thinking on the essential meaning of each word and on association between the words used. A similar exercise could be developed using the *haiku* – a short poem in Japanese style which consists of three lines: the first and third have five syllables and the middle line has seven.

The exploration is continued with an analysis of ideas associated with 'black' and then, possibly, with 'white and black' in combination, comparing and contrasting the symbolism, feelings and associations.

Third level planning

After thinking through possible questions to be explored and activities to be developed, the third level of planning is to research available resources which can be used. Fig. 12 below summarizes the avenues of possible exploration. Reference books are reviewed and selections compiled into annotated bibliographies. Books are judged on the quality of text and presentation. Reference books need to be detailed but not too technical, unless the technical terms are fully explained; they also need to be graded in difficulty. Fiction needs to be appropriate for the emotional and social level of the child, yet intellectually stimulating and imaginatively written.

Local expertise needs to be located, together with details of resources which are available in museums, records offices, libraries and exhibitions. Materials which have been commercially produced should also

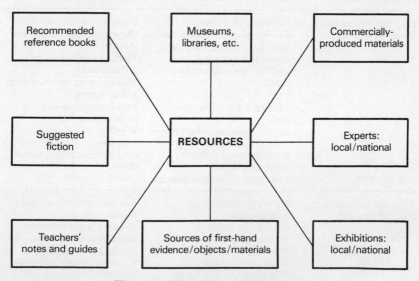

Fig. 12   Third level planning

be reviewed. These can be adapted or extended or sometimes used in the original form, although very few curriculum resources have been produced for exceptionally able pupils *per se*. Finally, detailed teachers' notes and guides may be needed, particularly if the project involves study in a new or unusual subject.

Planning a curriculum extension project for infant pupils (aged 6–7 years)

The project based on 'Colour' is designed for pupils aged eight to ten years but, using the same guidelines, the following project outline, 'Working with Dinosaurs' illustrates how the same principles are put into practice in developing an extension project for infant children. Barbara Bexley, headteacher of an infant school, together with her staff, devised the project.

The basic project assumed that all the children were fluent readers. Most of the children were of above average ability and some of them were highly able. Special attention was given to developing the skills of reading and number and to methods of recording which were succinct, relevant and of use to other children as a reference. All activities were developed in greater detail than is outlined here and the full project includes a list of extra resources, extensive teachers' notes, bibliography and useful addresses. The first level planning for the project is shown in Fig. 13, pp. 86–87.

Elaboration of activities

Possible questions	Suggested activities	Analysis of activities
How can dinosaurs names be classified?	*Collecting dinosaurs* Collect dinosaur names; see how many groups you can make. Identify similarities and find out meanings of words.	Research and library skills. Organizing and classifying information. Finding similarities and differences. Manipulating words, sorting and grouping.
	Making a dinosaur name game Divide dinosaur names into syllables. Make dinosaur name puzzles for other children to solve. Invent new dinosaur names.	Problem-posing and problem-solving. Working cooperatively. Imaginative thinking and development of fine motor skills.
What can you find out about dinosaurs?	*Carnivores/herbivores: habits/habitats* Group discussion to brainstorm possible questions: What did they eat? Where and how did they live?	Research and library skills. Discovering and reorganizing information logically and concisely. Analysing relationships. Comparing and evaluating scientific theories and data and drawing conclusions.

Possible questions	Suggested activities	Analysis of activities
	Establish a sequential method of finding out. Decide how results should be organized and recorded – Carroll diagram, Venn diagram, chart, decision tree, graph etc.	
When did dinosaurs live?	*Steps in time* Make a time-chart or comicstrip showing the stages of evolution.	Selecting relevant information and recording it to gain understanding.
How do scientists know what dinosaurs looked like?	*Skeletons* Prepare a full skeletal structure from a chicken carcass. Collect and identify animal bones. Bury bones in various soils and check regularly. Make a dinosaur skeleton puzzle. Make up a play about a dinosaur discovery.	Analysis of skeletal structure, discussion of the relationship of the parts contributing to the whole. Setting up experiments to test hypotheses. Manipulative and creative activity. Exploration of feelings through drama.
How big and how heavy were dinosaurs?	*Weighing and measuring the Megagiants: the heaviest, lightest, longest, shortest.* Collect information and decide how it should be organized and recorded. Make full-scale models/drawings of dinosaurs and yourself. Scale the models/drawings down.	Research for information. Ordering and presenting information logically. Analysing relationships. Measuring, counting, weighing.
	Gorgosaurus gifts! Build a dinosaur gift-shop. Make and sell 'dinosaur gifts'.	Imaginative, cooperative play. Inventing, creating, building.
	Dinosaur café/supermarket! Invent dinosaur food and build a café/supermarket. Design advertisements.	
What did dinosaurs sound like?	*Megalosaurus movement and Monoclonius music* Invent music which sounds like dinosaurs moving.	Creative expression through music, movement and drama.

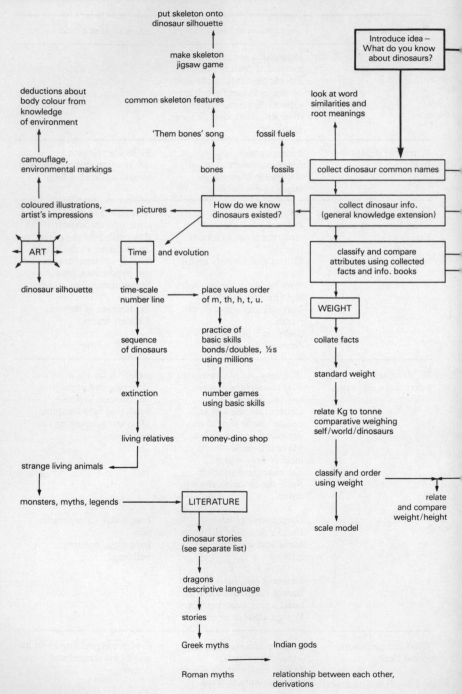

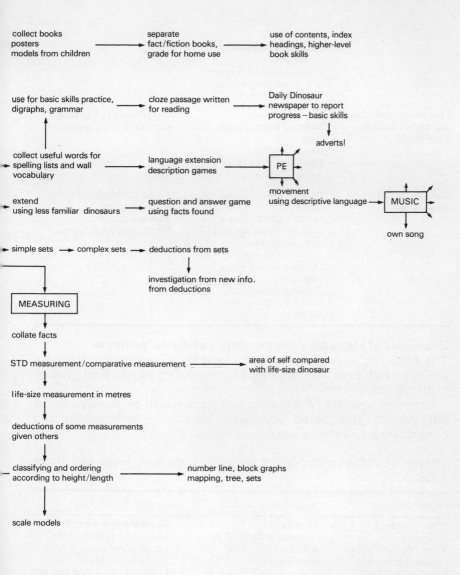

Fig. 13 'Dinosaurs': first level planning

	Move as if you were a dinosaur. Invent a play with music and movement to describe a dinosaur adventure.	
How many words can you find to describe dinosaurs?	*Dinosaur ditties* Make up a poem, story or song. *Animal alphabet* Invent words to make a dinosaur alphabet.	Development of language, expressing ideas creatively.
Can you make a dinosaur game?	*Prehistoric 'snakes and ladders'* Invent a game using a dinosaur landscape and dinosaur creatures. *An adventure game* Design a hazard game for explorers. *Bright pink dinosaurs* Create a technicolour dinosaur!	Using knowledge to create something new. Manipulative skills. Developing art and craft.

Examples of secondary curriculum extension projects

The following project outlines are examples of curriculum extension projects which have been developed for secondary pupils, aged thirteen to fifteen years.

Extensive notes for both teacher and pupil would be provided in the full project, plus useful addresses, sources of information and comprehensive bibliographies.

'*Aspects of Pollution*' (compiled by John Llewellyn Jones and Barry Adams)

Possible questions	Suggested activities	Analysis of activities
What is meant by pollution? When does a substance become a pollutant? Is pollution always man-made? What are considered the major problems of pollution in the twentieth century? What are the issues underlying pollution control?	*Air pollution* Chemical analysis of air pollution in the local environment. Monitoring the extent of grime deposits. Using lichens as pollution indicators. Study of the Warren Spring method of monitoring air pollution. *Soil pollution* Analysing impurities in the soil.	Application of scientific techniques to analyse the extent of pollution in the local environment. Organization of data into a logical and systematic record. Evaluation of evidence to draw conclusions. Creative thinking to suggest possible solutions. Testing of hypotheses, refinement and retesting. Evaluation.

	Testing for lead in soil and water.	Research of all available data.
	Testing for oil pollution.	Selecting key issues from complex information.
	Water pollution	
	Analysing impurities in water.	Analysing causes and implications. Suggesting alternatives.
	Animals as water pollution indicators.	
	Inquiry and/or debate on specific pollution incidents: Minemata, Lake Michigan, Seveso, myxomatosis.	Examining evidence, judging its validity. Analysis of cause and effect. Apportioning blame, making decisions, problem-solving.
	– What caused the damage?	
	– Who/what was to blame?	
	– What steps were taken or should have been taken to avert the damage?	
	– What steps should now be taken to prevent a recurrence of a similar incident?	
What recommendations would you make for the future?	Inquiry and/or debate on the global issue of the nature and control of pollution:	Anticipating effects and implications.
	– nuclear power	Looking to the future.
	– fuel and raw materials from urban waste.	Developing awareness and accepting responsibility for decision-making.

It is not possible to give the full range of activities in the following outlines but they do reveal the quality of the work and the depth of thinking which was undertaken quite easily by young secondary pupils.

'An Introduction to Genetic Engineering' (compiled by Davina Tweeddle)

Possible questions	Suggested activities	Analysis of activities
What is meant by the 'ladder of life'?	Making models of DNA structures.	Understanding the basic structure and acquiring the language of genetics.
What are the possible abuses of genetic engineering?	Study of recent research on genetic engineering. Debate of issues arising from the research, such as: What would happen if a new form of bacteria was accidentally developed which was resistant to antibiotics? it was decided to create a super-intelligent species? genetic engineering was seen as a solution to social ills?	Acquiring knowledge in order to discuss consequences and implications. Problem-posing and problem-solving. Examining major issues and evaluating ethical and moral values.

How can genetic engineering benefit mankind?	Analyse the worth of the following research projects: Production of human proteins and drugs important in medicine. Elimination of genetic diseases. Production of new substances to: improve waste disposal, increase crop yields, or develop bio-technology.	
What lines of research ought to be promoted and why?	Bacteria to extract metal from low grade ores? Male anti-fertility drug? Ethylene and propylene from enzyme action? Manufacture of oil? Animal food? More efficient photosynthesis? Intensification of nitrogen fixation?	Analysis of possible needs and avenues of exploration. Creative exploration of ideas. Judgment of values in the society.

'Medieval Studies' (compiled by Stephen Baines)

Possible questions	Suggested activities	Analysis of activities
What can be deduced about the differences between medieval and modern English?	*A study of medieval English* Study two parallel passages, one written in medieval English and the other in modern English. Find and account for all the similarities and differences, e.g. look for words which have changed their meanings or for words derived from French or Anglo-Saxon.	Analysis of complex language patterns. Classification and interpretation on the basis of logical reasoning and creative thinking.
What are the characteristics of good translation?	Compare and evaluate several translations of the same passage.	Evaluation based on justified literary criteria and personal values.
What were the general principles which guided the design and building of medieval castles?	*Medieval castle building* Design a medieval castle. Justify the design. Estimate the cost in money and manpower.	Research and library skills to gather knowledge about the designing and building of medieval castles. Organization of knowledge to prepare the basis for decision-making.

		Creative thinking based on knowledge acquired. Application of knowledge to problem-solving.
What responsibilities did the Lord of the Manor have in running his estate? What kinds of decisions did the Lord have to make? What problems faced a villein who lived on the estate?	*Running a medieval estate as Lord of the Manor* 1 A medieval farm is presented in simulation; the pupil must run the farm and make it viable. *Living as a villein on a medieval estate* 2 The pupil must live as a villein on the estate. Discuss the problems faced by (a) the Lord (b) the villein.	Assimilation of the complexity of medieval farming. Application of knowledge to problem-solving. Discussion and evaluation of the problems presented on the basis of ethical, economic and political grounds.

'Historical Detective Work' (compiled by Julian Whybra)

Possible questions	Suggested activities	Analysis of activities
Why do you think this military disaster occurred? Who do you think was responsible?	*The Battle of Isandhlwana, 1879* *The Zulu War* Using all available evidence – e.g. lists of army units at Isandhlwana, officers' order books, survivors' accounts, maps of the area – conduct an investigation to find out why the British army was annihilated and who was responsible.	Analysis of complex but incomplete information. Interpretation of primary historical evidence. Reasoned deduction to produce logical interpretation. Evaluation of people's supposed motives and intentions. Exploration of the meaning of responsibility and personal justification.
Is it possible to ascertain the nature of the Saxon settlement of England through a study of place-names?	*The Saxon settlement of England* Using maps, together with a study of place-name derivations, plot the apparent pattern of the Saxon settlement of an area of England. Observe and analyse any resultant pattern. Test any theory which may be derived by investigating the settlement of other areas in England.	Participation in original research. Testing an hypothesis. Development of greater understanding of the local environment. Analysis of complex information. Logical thinking based on evidence. Problem-solving.

How accurately can a family tree be traced using the National Registry of Births, Marriages and Deaths and Parish Registers of the Established Church of England?

Solving genealogical problems
Complete the 'X' family tree using the records available. Analyse the problems of inter-relating two known family trees.

Participation in genuine historical research.
Analysis of evidence through logic and calculated guesswork.
Problem-solving.
Using primary historical evidence as a basis for creative and evaluative thinking.

What can be learned about social life and values from these historical records?

Trace the varying nature of an individual's life over five centuries through an examination of, for example, the infant mortality rate, population movements, occupational changes, age of marriage, etc.

The four examples of secondary projects which have been outlined are mainly analytic and academic assignments, although many aspects of each also demand creative thinking. However, it is equally important to provide extension activities in other aspects of the curriculum, e.g. art, music, drama, craft and technology. It is also necessary to include physical and practical activities so that a balance of projects is provided.

Reference
[1]The first series of curriculum extension projects at infant, junior and secondary levels are available from Essex Education Authority.

Chapter 9

Organization and Personnel

In Chapters 7 and 8 we discussed the importance of building the higher-order thinking skills into normal class activities. We also looked at the need to move towards individualized learning programmes, develop appropriate questioning techniques and study skills which lead to independent learning, and to provide adequate resources to enable depth and breadth in individual research. However, we must also analyse the efficiency of various organizational strategies and examine why and how certain strategies can promote or inhibit a teacher's attempts to cater for individual needs and differences.

Leadership and cooperation

In any discussion about school organization, several points need to be underlined. Firstly, the leadership of the headteacher and senior staff is vital, since they will be responsible for the major administrative planning and supporting the staff. Adaptability, cooperation and flexibility are the key words which should underlie the planning of a school timetable, and the headteacher's role should be that of initiator, arbitrator and guide. However, planning, innovation and change should equally involve the teachers since they must be committed to making the system work to its fullest advantage, be aware of the purposes, advantages and weaknesses and realize that there can be no ideal arrangement which will solve all problems. Finally, parents also should be informed about what is happening and why. Time spent explaining and discussing at parents' meetings is time well spent and produces greater cooperation and understanding, together with a feeling of involvement.

Special schools or normal schools?

When provision for very able children is discussed, sometimes the issue is polarized between segregation through the provision of special schools and integration within the normal school. Both are inadequate solutions to the problem. A unique case could be made for special schools for music or ballet where early training is essential for the perfect mastery of exceptional skills; but even in these instances, an early decision about a child's future life and career requires that the child demonstrate unique ability and total singlemindedness at a very early age. Even then, the child's education should be as broad as possible not only to provide a truly liberal education but also to allow for a change of direction.

Other concerns which the issue of special schools raise are:

1   At what age would the selection be made? Would children of necessity be deprived of family life since such schools would need to be residential in order to be viable?
2   Bearing in mind the problems of identification, on what criteria would children be selected? Would it be by manifest ability? If so, what about children with potential as yet unrevealed due to lack of opportunity?
3   Would such schools develop all-round ability or be even more specialist and develop specific mathematical or scientific or literary abilities? What would happen to children who have a definite talent in one aspect of the curriculum but possibly not in others?
4   Would such an insular education allow a pupil to develop a true understanding of the society in which s/he lives and in which s/he will eventually play a vital role?

On the other hand, to talk about providing for very able children in the ordinary school is equally open to misinterpretation. To plead for integration and the development of the *well-rounded* individual can, and often does, disguise an education which promotes sameness and mediocrity. All children are unique individuals but very able children possess abilities which *accentuate* their differences when compared with others. The phrase 'well-rounded' implies uniformity, a compressing of interesting and even eccentric differences into a predictable pattern. How much better to plead for the enhancement of individual differences in an atmosphere of cooperation, mutual service and understanding!

The ideal solution is to strive for a compromise between the polarizations: education of pupils in a truly comprehensive system which not only allows for, but also consciously promotes, differentiation. A child aged seven who has mathematical ability comparable with older children needs to be allowed to do mathematics work with them; a child of eleven who has a special and advanced understanding of literature needs to discuss and share ideas with other like-minded, possibly older, children. It should be possible to allow groups of pupils to work together, on the basis of shared and comparable ability and interest, for extended periods of time.

Flexible grouping
It is often much easier to accommodate and develop this flexibility at primary level, since it is more common to find the school organization based on an integrated day where children can pursue an activity without a persistent, periodic and often disruptive bell. In the best

primary schools, the composition of groups is flexible. Sometimes pupils of mixed ability come together; sometimes groups are based on specific abilities or interests, regardless of chronological age.

It is important, however, at this point, to raise certain issues which need to be borne in mind when children work in groups, however flexible the overall organization might be. Mixed-ability groups demand flexible styles of teaching. It is quite paradoxical to gather together pupils who have widely different abilities and aptitudes and then to teach them as a homogeneous unit. Mixed-ability grouping demands group/individual activities which vary in pace, depth, breadth and approach. However, to assume that 'setting' children in broad ability bands is therefore necessarily the answer also poses difficulties. Setting might somewhat reduce the ability range, but the group is still a mixed-ability group. Moreover, very able children who are under-achieving, or who are troublesome or disruptive, are likely to be put into the lower sets which exacerbates their problems. So, once again, we are really discussing the quality of *teaching style*: although flexibility of school organization undoubtedly helps a teacher to be more creative in her approach, she must still hold an educational philosophy which seeks to promote the growth of the individual rather than one which seeks to promote uniformity.

It might be more difficult, initially, to develop greater flexibility at secondary level. The following suggestions may seem idealistic, but they are realistic in that they are possible, given good leadership and a willingness on the part of teachers to accept gradual and well-planned change.

Perhaps the first questions headteachers and teachers need to ask are:

1 Should the curriculum be a patchwork of supposedly unrelated items?
2 Do children learn best in a series of short disparate activities where, in the course of one day, the mind leaps from one concept to another, from one topic to another, from one teacher's idiosyncracies to another's?

Certainly, for very able children there is little time to explore anything in depth, to read anything at length or to pursue ideas to a conclusion. Their common reaction to curriculum extension activities, in which they pursue a topic for as long as three days, is one of exhilaration and deep personal satisfaction. Many express the wish for an even longer period devoted to one topic.

Teachers may argue that extended periods of study would be unsuitable for less able pupils, but it is not the *length of time* which would present problems, but the *kinds of activities* developed. Flexibility of teaching style and approach are the important issues. Instead of receiving waves of 30 pupils four to seven times a day, which exhausts both teacher and pupil, it would be so much easier to develop group and individual activities across a half day or even a full day. To take the idea even further, a programme of integrated study with team teaching would not only allow teachers to share their expertise but would also facilitate group withdrawal for specific purposes.

The ideal education, instead of being largely geared to a *content*-oriented syllabus, should, perhaps, be *skills* oriented, with a core curriculum to provide children with the necessary skills for independent learning, problem-posing and problem-solving. Public examinations could also be geared to problem-solving and taken whenever the child was ready, which would not necessarily be at one particular age nor would it entail all examinations being taken in the same year.

Even if the full accomplishment of such ideals constitutes a life-time's work, teachers can nevertheless begin to innovate and gradually move towards a system whereby they and their pupils are enabled to work in a more creative and flexible way.

Resources in the community

Education should be a matter of negotiation between teacher, child and parents. We need a synthesis of the professional skills of the teacher, the interests and abilities of the child, and the understanding and concern of the parents. But education should also involve leading the child to participate in and understand the community at large, and capitalize on the expertise and facilities within it.

There is a wealth of talent and resources available in local communities which merely needs to be organized, classified and catalogued and then made available to teachers and pupils. People in local industries, commerce, professions and societies have expertise and usually are only too willing to help. A very able child might find a mentor within the community who would share his/her knowledge, guide reading or discuss ideas, and be an essential outlet, a vital contact to promote and encourage a particular interest. Curators of museums, archivists and librarians can also be approached for help; museums and record offices store fascinating resources which are greatly under-used.

The problem, however, is often not so much one of finding resources within the community but of persuading teachers that a very able child can miss several days of conventional schooling and hardly notice it. A few moments of explanation would be sufficient to bridge the gap.

Parents, too, can be involved. With younger children, they might supervise group activities, chair discussions, transcribe or record in some other way for a child, help with model-making, or provide transport to and from an outside activity or visit. Older pupils could also benefit from discussion and exchange of ideas with parents who have specialist interests, knowledge or expertise. As early retirement increases, there are many adults with time and expertise who would enjoy providing such a service.

Extra-curricular activities

Many schools run extra-curricular clubs and societies which depend on teachers' personal interest and their willingness to devote extra time to such activities. These clubs are frequently a means whereby a very able child can develop personal hobbies such as magazine editing, chess, electronics, computer science, astronomy, drama, photography etc. Competitions and public exhibitions, pupils' writing, models, inventions, art and craft, together with relevant, useful community projects, help to provide outlets for young writers, inventors and artists and also establish within the school and the wider community, standards of excellence and *acceptance* of excellence. Challenges of this kind are essential so that the atmosphere within the school positively promotes and acknowledges high endeavour of all kinds.

Curriculum extension courses

Throughout the book, the emphasis has been on catering for the very able child in the normal school, but there have also been constant references to curriculum extension courses. In Essex, these courses serve two major functions. Firstly, they are the culmination of in-service programmes for teachers, during which curriculum extension projects are tried out and evaluated, and teachers gain experience of working with very able pupils. Secondly, the courses give very able pupils the opportunity to work together, a necessary and beneficial experience which, as we have seen, the children find both stimulating and reassuring.

Such courses can be residential or day courses. Several schools might pool their expertise and share the preparation and organization. Pupils sometimes meet together twice a term or once a week to pursue a project and exchange ideas. When very able pupils are given the opportunity to work together, they often teach one another through stimulating new ideas, sharing problem-solving assignments, wrestling with complexities and challenging each other's opinions and hypotheses. They, themselves, can be the greatest resource we have, if only teachers could create the appropriate opportunities for pupils to share and use their abilities in this way. Apart from the intellectual satisfaction derived from exchanging ideas with other pupils, many very able children *need* the emotional and social contact with like-minded peers to reassure themselves that they are normal.

The following quotations are taken from pupils' evaluations of curriculum extension courses. Their comments speak for themselves and clearly indicate their needs, frustrations and gentle good humour and tolerance!

One thing I have found out is that I'm not the only idiot with a weird sense of humour. For the first time I found it easy to make friends – people of my own age understand what I'm talking about – I enjoy arguing about something – and here I've had great practice at it!

The most enjoyable aspect was having to think for yourself. In school, you work mostly from textbooks and, in history for example, you are presented with other people's ideas. Here we are given primary source material and you had to work it out for yourself. Looking at the original documents in Ingatestone (a local museum) was fascinating!

I have been away from the repetition of school – I didn't have to wait for people to catch up – I could go off on my own train of thought. I could work as fast as I could. Of course, the pupil-teacher ratio was ideal – and I do understand the difficulties of teachers with large classes – but if we could come on these courses more often – I for one would greatly benefit.

Before I came on this course, I thought I was out on my own. By this I mean that I would never find a person of the same ability who could communicate with me on the same level. I am glad to say that I have now found not one but 27 of them. Now that I have found these people, a lot of worry and depression has been lifted off my mind and consequently I have changed, for before I never quite believed in myself or my eventual purpose in life (which will remain a secret) and now I do.

It was super to talk to teachers as adults – you could really ask them important questions but still criticize their ideas. They can be regarded as over-age children and friends.

The whole concept of bringing people together in small groups to study something of common interest is fantastic. Obviously the teachers had put a lot of effort into making the course more enjoyable by actually sitting down and thinking 'Will they find this interesting?'

P.S. I enjoyed having to work for once.
P.P.S. The most phenomenal success of the course was Medieval Studies which was ridiculously difficult, aggravating and perversely addictive!
P.P.P.S. Star-power was the most stimulating and sinister game I have ever come across.
P.P.P.P.S. Can I come again? I don't know anyone else who can fight off a Zulu attack whilst running a medieval farm single-handed and playing 3D hexagonal chess in his mind!

In Essex pupils and teachers evaluate the curriculum extension courses and one of the most salutary and moving realizations which has emerged from such discussions is that many very able pupils understand the teacher's dilemma in the classroom. They are aware of the many demands and pressures and express their sympathy by deliberately refraining from increasing them. It is common for a pupil to say, 'They (the teachers) do their best in a very difficult situation.' They admit to accepting a routine which seldom challenges or excites them and we, as teachers, often fail to realize and appreciate the level of their understanding and consideration.

A young man, of fourteen years of age, chose to write a poem at the end of a curriculum extension course. Although the poem reveals despair and frustration, he was determined to overcome the problem he encountered. His message lies in the first letter of each line!

Lost and alone
Elated for one week, only
To drown in depression
Sucked beneath the waves of pleasure
Hypercriticized by many
Appeased by few
Veneered by acceptance
Endangered by mine own wants
Attributed with abnormality and
Retributed for so much
Everywhere people talk but don't
Understand the inner experience
Null and void in reality
In super imposed creations
Open and marked
Nothing comprehends my intentions
Parted from loves and ecstasy
Arranged again in line
Resigned to
Trudge the weary path only to see the repetition of
Yesterday.
      BUT, *I am not alone!*

Providing opportunities for very able pupils to participate in such courses is not so much a matter of extensive additional finance but of organization. There are many teachers who have considerable subject expertise, or a particular interest, who have a great deal to contribute to a curriculum extension course. The expertise within the community can be used and, if several schools can cooperate and share the preparation and organization, resources and facilities can also be shared.

Posts of special responsibility

Subject or faculty leadership through heads of departments has long been accepted in secondary schools, and has recently grown in primary schools as a means of effective teacher guidance and support. Although every teacher should be concerned with counselling pupils, or catering for the needs of pupils with learning difficulties, special posts of responsibility have been created in both of these areas. Schools have appointed heads of pastoral care and heads of remedial education so that effort can be coordinated and expertise shared. The same reasons justify the appointment of a teacher to take a leadership role in meeting the needs of very able pupils. Of course, every teacher should be aware and concerned, but there is strength in a central source of guidance and coordination when one teacher takes ultimate responsibility. Such a teacher could be concerned with evaluating and developing assessment procedures, training other staff, discussing problems and liaising with teachers, parents and the school to which the child moves on. It is essential to monitor the progress of very able pupils and to keep careful and detailed records of curriculum extension work. Such a person could organize curriculum extension courses, liaise with other schools, locate and acquire special resources and be the focal point for contact and general guidance.

Such localized activity should be generally coordinated by a person in an overall advisory capacity within an area. The general adviser would lead in-service education courses, identify good practice, promote cooperative activity, disseminate information, gather resources centrally and be available to give advice and support to schools. The adviser could also discuss strategies of curriculum extension, coordinate the expertise available within the area, guide the preparation of curriculum extension materials in teacher workshops and advise on problems of individual pupils in schools.

Eventually, we might hope for a small team of specialist peripatetic teachers who could organize regular withdrawal classes for those pupils who need even more than the best school can provide.

Conclusion

Education should be exciting and relevant for *all* children, and paying attention to the special needs of very able children is one part of putting this principle into practice. The techniques for identifying very able children improve teachers' skills in assessing *all* children's needs. Extending the depth and breadth of curriculum activities in schools increases opportunity for *all* children and possibly raises the ceiling of attainment for all children as a result.

In many instances, we have been discussing and promoting accepted ideals in education. Where we have differed is in concentrating on a minority group of pupils who have been largely misunderstood and ignored but could be the leaders of tomorrow. Parents and teachers must try therefore to ensure that such leadership emanates from the base of wisdom and humanity, that such skills and insight are used constructively and positively for the benefit both of the individuals and the community.

Accepting the obviously essential role of parents, the additional key figure must be the teacher, for it is she who can transform a Gradgrindian classroom into an adventure playground. The personality of the teacher, her philosophy, sensitivity, dedication and professionalism, act as the catalyst to promote and develop the best within the child. Most pupils remember only a fraction of *what* they learned at school. What they do remember vividly, however, is the teacher who inspired them to go on learning, who made learning exciting, who extended horizons and fed the flame of curiosity.

However, a teacher cannot function effectively without good initial training and continued in-service support. The effects of present financial cuts in education are resulting in inadequate resources, depleted in-service courses and lowered morale. How are teachers to provide an A-grade education with such E-grade resources?

'Equality of opportunity' is the current gospel of education, and one which I fully endorse. However, equality of opportunity does not mean that all children have the same abilities and can learn the same things in the same way at the same time. Nor does it mean uniformity of attainment and the neglect of the pursuit of excellence.

THE APPENDIXES

Appendix A

The History and Development of Work with Gifted Children in Essex

A brief description of the historical background to the Essex programme for exceptionally able pupils which also gives an outline of the current programme which has provided the base of experience and knowledge which underlies this book.

Gifted Children and the Brentwood Experiment[1] by Sidney Bridges is, by now, a well-known account of the first work with gifted children in the county of Essex. Bridges was concerned to provide students in initial training with experience in working with gifted children. He wanted the students to realize, at first hand, the capabilities of very able pupils and to begin to develop an understanding of their needs.

The Brentwood Institute of Higher Education is situated in an area in which pupils could (and still can) take a verbal-reasoning test in the fourth year of the junior school for entrance into a grammar school. Bridges initially selected twenty pupils who had scored over 130 on a verbal-reasoning 11 + selective test and they were invited to the college for one afternoon a week. During that time, the children studied nature study, physics, chemistry, mathematics, art and craft. Students were asked to volunteer for participation in the project since Bridges' aim was to develop students' understanding of the needs of very able pupils. However, it was soon realized that the students were not sufficiently experienced to be able to be flexible in their approach, nor had they yet acquired adequate depth and breadth of knowledge in their subjects or disciplines. Far more support and guidance from tutors was needed than had been originally realized.

Another major realization was that the school achievement of the pupils did not match their potential and that: 'The children had long since become accustomed to a certain level of expectation on the part of their teachers, and probably of their parents. The result was that, on the whole, their level of aspiration or demands upon themselves was relatively low.'[2] In addition, many of the children found it difficult to sustain concentration. It seemed that they had become so accustomed to working rapidly but superficially that they had failed to develop the habits of perseverance needed for rigorous study.

Consequently, the next phase of the project was structured differently. Bridges decided to select a younger group of children in order to work with them over a period of two or three years, firstly to find out if younger pupils were also similarly conditioned to respond to low school expectation, and secondly to see if that expectation could be changed. College tutors were to be involved to a much greater extent in both the preparation of courses and the teaching of the children. Children were to meet at the college one afternoon each week. Mr George Robb, County Psychologist and a founder member of the National Association of Gifted Children, was invited to help. Robb organized testing in several schools using the Stanford-Binet Intelligence Test,[3] and thirty pupils were selected, each with an IQ score of 140+. The group consisted of 17 nine-year-olds and 21 eight-year-olds. All pupils were exceptional in reading and language and most came from homes of high socio-economic status.

After three years' work, Bridges suggested that even the younger pupils had already accepted the low expectations of many of their teachers. He found that, although teachers may have recognized that certain of the pupils were exceptionally able, they were largely unaware of the *real* capacity of these pupils. Consequently, many of the pupils could be regarded as under-achievers and, indeed, in group discussions, many of the pupils expressed their feeling of boredom at school. They usually finished their work long before other children and found much of it very easy. In 1980, another experiment with gifted children was set up in the North-East Division of Essex. Mr George Robb, County Psychologist, Mr Terence Carter, Area Education Officer, and several county inspectors were involved. Pupils from the second year of the junior schools were selected on the basis of individual assessment carried out by the School Psychological Service, and the pupils' IQiq scores ranged from 135–160+. Four classes, each containing from four to seven pupils, were set up and pupils met twice a week in local secondary schools. Classes, which were held twice a week for two years, were taken by parents who were specialists in science, maths or biology.

Some important lessons were learned from this experiment. Firstly, as in the Brentwood experiment, the children certainly enjoyed the experience of working together, and the challenge of working with like minds was often a salutary one. Secondly, teachers were very anxious to be involved and wanted to be kept informed of what was happening. They were not generally in favour of curriculum extension which was completely divorced from the rest of the children's school experience.

The third phase of the Essex project began with a day conference for teachers in 1971 on 'The Needs of the Exceptional Child'. A working party of eight primary and secondary teachers was formed under the chairmanship of Mrs Susan Roberts, an educational psychologist. The working party was given permission to run an annual five-day residential course for primary children. Schools throughout Essex were invited to nominate children, aged between eight and ten years, who were tested by the educational psychologists, and pupils who scored over 140 on the Wechsler Scale of Intelligence[4] were accepted. The courses gradually became known as the 'Brooklands' courses since that was the name of the residential centre where they were held.

The working party organized its first residential course in the summer of 1972 and the teachers involved were asked to observe and study the characteristics and needs of the pupils who participated. It was undoubtedly a vital and exciting learning experience for the teachers. Schemes of work were prepared under the following general guidelines:

1   Projects of work were to be generated from problem-posing;
2   Pupils were to be encouraged to work through group discussion;
3   Pupils were to lead the course of the exploration;
4   Teachers and pupils were to be co-learners.

By 1975, the teachers who were involved in preparing the courses felt that they could begin to discuss the needs of very able children, comment on the pupils' learning styles and document some of their ideas for curriculum extension projects for other teachers to use in schools.

In the summer of 1978, residential courses began for secondary pupils aged thirteen to fourteen years, and in September 1978, I took up the newly-created post of County Advisory Teacher for Exceptionally Able Children. The role of the advisory teacher was to:

1   Develop teacher awareness of the needs of exceptionally able pupils;
2   Develop skills in identification techniques which could be used in classrooms;
3   Coordinate County expertise;
4   Provide a support service for schools, giving guidance on individual pupils and curriculum extension.

In practice, the work has involved organizing teacher workshops on identification strategies and curriculum provision, running curriculum extension courses for pupils and teachers (day and residential), visiting schools to discuss the particular problems of teachers, pupils and parents, and building a collection of resource materials for classroom use.

References
[1]BRIDGES, S. (1969) *Gifted Children and the Brentwood Experiment* London: Pitman
[2]ibid.
[3]The Stanford-Binet Intelligence Test is an individual test of intelligence (revised 1972, Boston: Houghton-Mifflin). The test measures skills in seven categories:
   language – naming objects and defining words;

reasoning – pointing out an absurdity;
memory – remembering sentences and digits;
conceptual – explaining meanings;
social intelligence – understanding social identities;
numerical reasoning – problem-solving;
visual-motor – copying forms.

[4]The Wechsler Scale of Intelligence is an individualized test of intelligence. It is discussed in detail on p. 57.

Appendix B

The Development of Creative Mathematical Ability in the Early Years

Hilda Taylor

Hilda Taylor is a headmistress of an infant school (pupils 5–7+ years of age). Her special interest is mathematics and she describes the characteristics of young children who manifest a particularly creative perception of mathematical concepts. Miss Taylor's creative approach to the teaching of mathematics and her style of questioning encourages children to explore, to find their own explanations and to draw their own conclusions. Her descriptions of the children and their thoughts reflect her own obvious understanding and care. The individualized approach allows children to work at varying levels according to their abilities.

> Your children are not your children . . .
> And though they are with you they belong not to you . . .
> *For they have their own thoughts . . .*
> For life goes not backward nor tarries with yesterday . . .
> You are the bows from which your children as living arrows are sent forth . . .

The Prophet Kahlil Gibran[1]

During my initial training a tutor made a comment which I have had cause to remember on many occasions since. She said, 'You will meet some children who, potentially, are far more intelligent than you are.' She might have added, '. . . and some may be far more creative and divergent in thinking than you are.'

I have certainly found this to be true, but while a teacher may be faced with what seems to be an alarming sense of responsibility for such children, some situations provide an exciting, stimulating opportunity for the creative development of a teacher. It is important, though, to accept one's own limitations and to be honest with children. A little girl once said to me, 'When you were six, could you draw as well as I can?' My truthful, rueful answer had to be, 'No, and I can't draw as well as you can now.'

I have come to believe that the making of mathematics is essentially a creative act, akin to the making of a picture, or of music, or of a poem. I believe passionately that children must be released from a fear of failure and a dread of making mistakes which unfortunately dogged my own early attempts in mathematics. They need *time* and freedom to explore a situation in order to develop the intuitive and reflective capacities necessary for mathematical thought. Trial necessarily involves the possibility of error and this must be understood and accepted as non-threatening.

Mathematical learning has deep emotional roots. Caldwell[2] considers that mathematics is a form of self-analysis because it necessitates contemplative introspection. Skemp[3] states that 'accelerated learning' is related to the 'process of creation of the inner self' or 'entelechy'. Perhaps the creative aspect of mathematics is appreciated most readily in activities which are both mathematical and artistic.

A group of infant children were given pieces of card and invited to rotate and draw each shape. Lindsey selected a piece which reminded her of a cat. The children worked and talked and ultimately Lindsey wrote:

This cat looks like it is vibrating.
It looks like it's been twanged.
Also I think it looks like a sunflower.
Dawn thinks it looks like a wheel.
Emily thinks it is intersecting.
Sarah said it looks like a catherine wheel.
Emily also thought it looks like a ball of wool.

Dawn wrote:

I used a circle.
My circle made a ball.
My circle shape makes a wheel.
It looks like a ball of wool.
It looks like a big doughnut.
It looks like the world.
It looks like a polo.
It has got lots of rings in it.

Kamini had been shown how to make a tetrahedron by folding four circles to produce triangular faces which were then assembled to produce the required three-dimensional shape. When the other children in her group left for the midday meal Kamini continued to work for a further twenty minutes. She returned to her self-appointed task in the afternoon. She said, 'I want to investigate how these shapes will fit together. I think five might.' As she produced the tetrahedra she said, 'I expect the first person who made a tetrahedron would have to investigate how it might go. They wouldn't know. I didn't know but ... it's a happy ending.' Later she gathered small groups of children together within her class and taught them the newly-acquired skill. She was sensitively aware of the limitations of a retarded child in the class and spoke quietly to her teacher about it: 'I don't know what I shall do if A wants to make one.' Her teacher said, 'You must help her, as I do.'

Children need to work together and to help one another and it is a teacher's responsibility not only to nurture intellectual abilities but also to create a climate of care and cooperation amongst children of very different abilities. Fostering exceptional ability in children should never involve the encouragement of competitive arrogance and invidious comparisons but it is equally wrong to pretend that differences do not exist. John, for example, was considered to be an 'expert' in mathematical model-making and the children accepted his exceptional ability and elected him an ancillary teacher on many occasions.

Papert[4] argues that, so far as possible, mathematics should be learned within a natural, meaningful context as a child learns his native language. Whenever appropriate, therefore, integrated, thematic situations should be exploited for mathematical investigation. Such opportunities may arise unexpectedly. The trampoline (nursery size) cord needed to be replaced and a group of children were asked to find out the length of cord needed. Various recordings were made. The children were then asked: 'If ever we need a new mat for the centre how can we find out the measurement of *this* (indicated by movement of hand) surface?' Several suggestions were made:

STEFAN (indicating length and breadth) You could measure down there and across there.

TEACHER What about the other parts you haven't touched?

STEFAN (drawing his finger swiftly to and fro) You could measure a lot of lines, like that.

Eventually the teacher produced a pile of small books.

TEACHER Let's cover the surface with these Bronto books.

The children covered the surface.

TEACHER That's all right. There are no books overlapping and no spaces between them but *these* books at the side come over the edge. What can we do about that?

Pause whilst the children pondered about this.

JANET I know. Why don't we get some Bronto-book size pieces of paper and cover the space? When we get to the side we can cut them up like pieces of jigsaw and fit them together.

The children needed no further help!

The work was taken into another classroom and discussion centred upon whether or not there was a difference between the inside and outside measurement of the trampoline frame. Working in pairs, six children were given 'running tracks'.

TEACHER   What can you say about the runner on the inside of the track and the runner on the outside of the track?
ALICE   (instant response) An outside runner would need a headstart.

Later she wrote 'I found out a lot. The perimeter is 166 cm inside. The outside is 203 cm. I count(ed) in tens. ... The difference is 37 cm.' Darren wrote: 'I took 166 out of the base ten (set) and built up to 203.'

I have found that children do not learn best in what has been called a 'cafeteria of experience' or a 'wet playtime all day'. A teacher has a responsibility to create the necessary structures whereby children can learn through organized constraints to exercise self-disciplined freedom. Discoveries cannot be made in a vacuum.

Referring to Mednick's associationist theory of creativity Ogilvie states: '... an individual without the requisite elements in his response repertoire can hardly be expected to combine them in a creative solution: a child who has not learned his numbers will never combine them in novel number series ...'

When Jonathan (Jon) came to school at five he had already been encouraged to look at the world as a mathematician and was accomplished in mental computational skills far beyond the level of most infant school children. Along with other able children he was learning how to deal with percentages and decimals when he was six-and-a-half years of age. He had been taught how to cut out a hundred squares and colour 50, 25, 75 per cent which was relatively simple for him. He was then asked, 'What do you think $33\frac{1}{3}$ per cent would be?' The response was immediate: 'A third, because 3×33 makes 99 and another one, split that into three – yes, a third.'

Later, when he had been introduced to the first place of decimals, again using squared paper, the following exchange took place.

TEACHER   You know that 0·1 is 1/10th. What do you think 0·01 might be?
JON   Would it be 1/20th?
TEACHER   Come on, Jon, you understand base ten better than that!
JON   Oh yes, of course, a tenth of a tenth, 1/100th.

Paul and Stephen often *worked together* on mathematical problems and had no difficulty in producing a sequence of triangular numbers. They were asked: 'Can you put your sets together to make square numbers?' Stephen replied: 'Oh yes, like this. (Pause for action.) You put each one with one of the next size.'

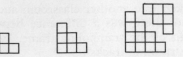

In order to help even the brightest children to understand the relative value of number powers, provision of suitable apparatus and basic teaching of these structures is essential.

Gillian had developed an extensive 'association reservoir' upon which to draw when she was involved in number operations in base three, using different inputs in a 10 for 1 (multiplication or ratio) 'machine'. A puzzled adult onlooker asked:

'Tell me what you are doing. I don't know what you are doing – ten for one, ten for one.'

Gillian was equally puzzled because the operation had become obvious for her. She replied:

'Ten? Ten? You can't have a ten in base three!'

She picked up a base piece (first grouping) and said, 'It's *this*.'

The following examples have been selected to demonstrate firstly, the importance of teacher questioning and secondly, the quality of the child's perception. In identifying children with exceptional ability, it is the quality of their insight, the speed of their perception, their ability to see possibilities and connections which are the vital clues. It is essential that such children are given opportunities to think, to talk and to experiment, with the teacher gently prompting to nudge the child further.

A group of children were playing the Dienes game, 'Apples on a tree'.[6] Working in pairs on individual logical trees the children used counters which they moved to each junction of the branches according to a throw of a die upon which appropriate base numerals were printed. They drew an apple as they reached the top of each branch. The best quality were nearest to the sun. After a prescribed number of throws the children decided which player had the best apples. Red crayons were given so that the children could draw apples. Louise immediately went to the crayon box and gave out green crayons also. She explained: 'The apples furthest from the sun should be green.' The apples she drew on the middle branches of her tree were half red and half green. It would seem that she had realized intuitively the relative value of the different positions. The children soon appreciated that the first throw of a die could determine the final outcome of the game.

The game 'Threeland' is a favourite with some children. They are given a pile of token 'coins' and asked to exchange them according to the rule that there must be no more than two of each colour in a column. Three are exchanged for a coin of the next colour on the left. Each child arranges the 'coins' on a grid so that mutual comparisons can be made. Kieran's far left column was purple.

KIERAN   What happens if I have three purple?
TEACHER   Think it out.
KIERAN   I could stick another strip of paper here (indicating left).
TEACHER   It could go on.
KIERAN   Yes, it could go on till you die.

This glimpse of infinity excited him.

Pre-Christmas multibase activities involved art and craft and children produced friezes to illustrate:

Base three   Three snowmen in one line
              Three lines in one park

Base four   Four gifts in one sock
              Four socks in one sack
              Four sacks on one sleigh

Base five   Five baubles on one tree
              Five trees on one shelf
              Five shelves in one shop

Base six   Six mince pies on one plate
              Six plates on one tray
              Six trays on one table

The children understood each individual piece of work but, as expected, most could make no connection between them. Victoria grasped the underlying mathematical structure. She was asked: 'What would be equivalent to the table if we built base six with cubes?' Her response was immediate: 'A third grouping – a big cube.' The multi-embodiments enabled her to make a rapid generalization which is unusual for an infant child.

A group of children were asked if they could produce a variety of shapes on a geo-board. If some were not possible they were asked to try to explain why not. This task proved to be very difficult for most children although they tried very hard. One shape was a non-square rhombus. I thought that the children were frustrated and confused and I apologized to them. Marek (sic) kindly said: 'Oh, don't worry, that's all right.'

During the afternoon, using their own initiative, Marek and his friends worked together in a corner of the classroom. They borrowed a stapler from the teacher and folded pieces of paper until they were satisfied that each had produced a non-square rhombus. The children brought the shapes to me with considerable delight and satisfaction. They had used the initial activity as a stimulus for their own purposes. They were able to discuss the angles of their shapes and to comment upon the way in which they differed from the angles of a square, using terms such as, 'larger than', 'smaller than', 'squashed up' and so on.

This made me realize that as teachers we often underestimate the capabilities of children and fail to give them the opportunity for independent problem solving.

A group of rising-sevens were given a sheet of paper and shown how to fold it into sixteen equal parts. The children counted the spaces and quickly found that there were sixteen – four sets of four in each direction. They were then given instructions as follows:

Choose four colours for jumpers.
Choose four colours for trousers or skirts.
Make a code.

Stephen's choice was as follows:

| *Jumpers* | Red | light green | blue | yellow |
| *Trousers* | White | dark green | black | pink |

The instructions continued:

Skirt/trouser colours may not be used for jumpers.
Jumper colours may not be used for skirts or trousers.
Draw an outfit – jumper and trousers (or skirt) in each space.
You may use the same colour more than once but you must not have the same outfit more than once or the same colours together more than once.

When the instructions were understood the children proceeded to draw and, apart from Stephen, they used a random, trial and error method, as might be expected. There were many mistakes because the children found it difficult to consider all the rules at once. Stephen drew one outfit and immediately called to the teacher: 'I've got it. You use all the trouser colours that way [horizontally] and all the jumper colours the other way [vertically]!'

Along with other children, Stephen had been taught how to structure systems of sets. Stephen and Paul produced a system using attributes of summer time (see Fig. AB1, p. 115).

They had no difficulty in labelling a logical tree and assembled the elements of their sets at the ends of the branches.

Using a dictionary code, which they produced with very little help, the two boys related each set to a base four element and were able to count from left to right in base four.

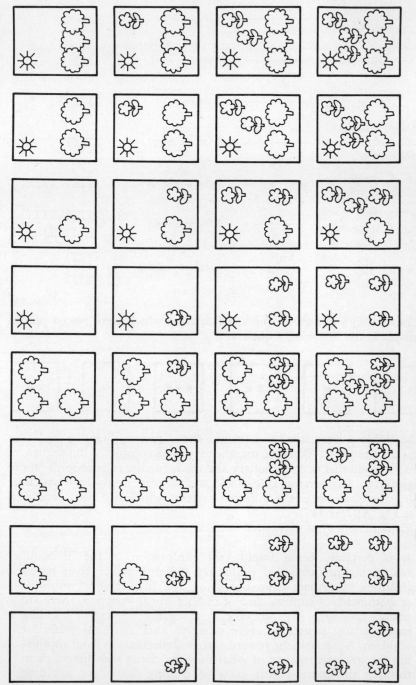

Fig. AB1   A system of sets using attributes of summer time

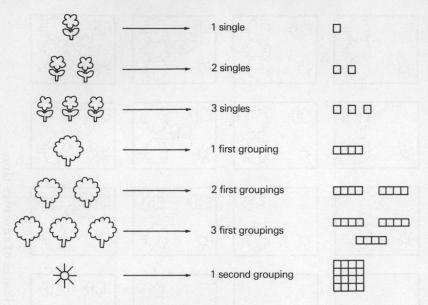

Later they were shown pieces of card on which were placed plastic squares in the following sequence:

The children were asked to continue the sequence. Stephen said: 'Ah yes, it's base four.' Working together the boys completed the sequence, produced another code dictionary and made further relationships on the logical tree. Stephen was able to add and subtract mentally in base four using the elements in the different systems which had been produced (see Fig. AB2, p. 117).

Zoltan Dienes has written:

It is certainly being found that exploration of the 'difficult' underlying mathematical structures delights rather than repels children. ... Apart from observing the principles of multiple embodiment, of contrast and of mathematical variation, there are many other steps we can take to make the process of learning mathematical structures more effective and more enjoyable for children. A punishment/reward system deflects them from appraising the intrinsic interest of what they are doing and directs them towards the more selfish ends of gaining favour or avoiding

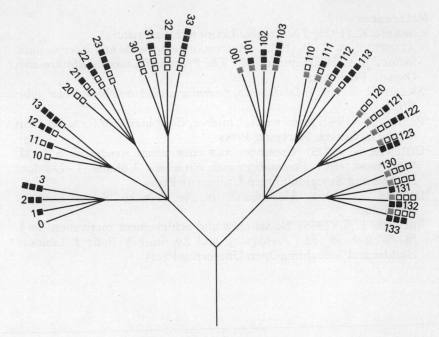

Fig. AB2   A logical tree

disfavour. We could do a great deal for our children's ethical as well as intellectual development by doing away with rewards and punishments, and substituting as intrinsic motivation the interest of the task itself. It is quite surprising how children will take an interest in unravelling abstract structures and their properties without any extrinsic push being necessary.[6]

Bruner's view does not exclude motivation but he writes: '... External reinforcement may indeed get a particular act going and may even lead to its repetition, but it does not nourish, reliably, the long course of learning by which man slowly builds in his own way a serviceable model of what the world is and what it can be.'[7] I believe this to be true. Often children are motivated by sharing an experience with each other and with a teacher. Often they want their achievement to be recognized by someone else. Nevertheless, there are occasions when a teacher may be in the way and children are able to work beyond praise or blame. As Dienes has found, young able mathematicians are capable of sustained, concentrated investigation of mathematical structures and take delight in their logic and elegance.

References

[1]GIBRAN, K. (1923) *The Prophet* London: Heinemann

[2]CALDWELL, A. K. P. (1972) 'Motivation, emotional and interpersonal factors' in L. R. Chapman (ed.) *The Process of Learning Mathematics* Oxford: Pergamon

[3]SKEMP, R. R. (1979) *Intelligence, Learning and Action* New York: John Wiley

[4]PAPERT, S. (1980) *Mindstorms, Children, Computers and Powerful Ideas* Brighton, Sussex: Harvester Press

[5]OGILVIE, E. (1975) 'Creativity and curriculum structure' in J. M. Whitehead (ed.) *Personality and Structure* Volume 1 London: Hodder and Stoughton/Open University Press

[6]DIENES, Z. (1964) *Mathematics in the Primary School* London: Macmillan

[7]BRUNER, J. S. (1975) 'Social class and achievement motivation' in J. M. Whitehead (ed.) *Personality and Learning* Volume 1 London: Hodder and Stoughton/Open University Press

Appendix C

Catering for the Very Able Child in the Infant School

Barbara Bexley

Barbara Bexley is headmistress of an infant school (pupils aged 5 to 7+ years). Although she is deeply concerned for all her pupils, she has played a very active role in developing curriculum extension materials for very able children. She believes in developing cooperation between teachers and parents so as to use the strengths of each. She is particularly interested in promoting creative thinking and problem-solving. Here she discusses the importance of detailed classroom observation and presents a number of interesting case studies.

'Look at them daffodils, Miss,' observed young Henry, indicating a flock of seagulls landing on the grass outside the classroom window. Meanwhile Tanya commented on her 'best ever weekend'. On Sunday morning, she had opted to watch a science programme on video, with 'a nice cup of coffee'. When she did not fully understand the reference to Pythagoras' theorem, her parents together with seven-year-old brother and four-year-old sister, had cut up squares of paper, and now she was pleased that she understood Pythagoras completely, hypotenuse and all!

These illustrations typify the range of ability found within our infant school. Both children are just six years old, one from an emotionally disturbed and inadequate home, the other obviously very able with interested and articulate parents. Both children are in the same class with 29 others, all individual people and with varying abilities. So what does the one teacher do?

Perhaps the first essential is to clarify the aim of infant teaching. A class of 30 children start school at 4+ years old, and it is probably their first introduction to formal education; but in those preceding years, they have learned a great deal and infant school education must be regarded as a continuation of the child's education and not as the beginning of it. Having accepted that, from which point do we continue? Starting school is often a shock for young children, however well prepared they are. I well remember, early in my career, a reception child who seemed somewhat dazed by school, and it was only after a month and a chance comment from his mother that I discovered that the child could read fluently. The shock of finding that he was not 'normal' had been very disturbing for him and consequently he had retired into a quiet, bewildered shell.

It is essential, therefore, to assess the child's level of attainment as soon as possible, and in an activity-based reception class, this can be accomplished if the teacher deliberately creates opportunities so that a child can reveal his/her abilities. The teacher needs to be able to assess the following:

Language fluency Given a picture to talk about, what is the quality of the child's language? Are adjectives and adverbs used in long sentences or does the child respond in single words or short phrases?

Sequencing, deducing, predicting Given a series of pictures, can the child order them to make a sequence story? Does s/he notice the mistakes given a 'What's wrong' picture? Does s/he find this test funny or a waste of time? Shown only a small section of a complete picture, can s/he predict the whole content?

Mathematical concepts How much of the rote number patterns that s/he chants are understood? Has s/he sorted out colour and shape names, and can s/he classify items into simple sets? Can s/he order in size or by weight?

Writing Can the child write his/her own name? Is s/he left- or right-handed?

Reading Using the Marie Clay *Concepts of Print* test,[1] does the child 'read' from left to right or recognize that the print is upside down, or that syllables are in juxtaposition? Does s/he understand the vocabulary of reading, i.e. letter, word, sentence, page, etc?

Such tests do not need numerical scoring but are more useful with the teacher's comments about the child's response written against each item. Apart from the Marie Clay test, all the other materials are available as part of the normal classroom equipment, and consist of LDA[2] picture cards, logic blocks, unifix cubes and small toys and shapes used for sorting. By testing all the children, the teacher should then be able to assess and group the children according to their acquired knowledge of mathematical and language concepts, and she should become aware of all children's needs, including the very able. For the majority of children, normal reception practice will then ensue, giving pre-reading experience to those who need it but allowing those with good reading concepts to make a start on formal reading activities. For the low-ability child, special provision will have to be made with the remedial teacher. Special provision must also be made for the child with exceptionally high ability, although this will inevitably have to rely on the classroom teacher.

In some cases it may be advisable, after a first term in the reception room, to consider accelerating the very bright child into the middle school. Rising fives are very egocentric and demanding, and much of the teacher's time will be taken up with teaching very basic skills. Whilst reading material for the young able reader can be acquired from other rooms, the general curriculum content may not be challenging enough for a good reader amongst non-readers. Any transfer should be considered carefully in the context of the child's social maturity and his/her relationship with the peer group. Watching free play at breaktimes is often an indicator of social adjustment. The attitude of the other staff should also be taken into account – a sympathetic teacher is more important than the classroom or its members.

Sympathy, stimulation and challenge would seem to be the most important factors in easing a bright child through the early years of school. Sympathy starts with realizing that however intellectually able the child is, s/he is still only a child and will sometimes exhibit behaviour that seems out of context. Baby habits may continue, and some very able children still seem to need the comfort of sucking a thumb, a strand of hair or clothing. Their logic may also be contradictory: for example, while a very able five-year-old explained the processes involved in space travel, he also insisted on the reality of the tooth fairy.

While many very able children learn to read early, some cannot read when they come to school. At a crucial time when the absorption process should have started, the child may have been in an emotionally unstable environment, may have experienced periods of ill-health or may have been in a deprived home. However, when given the appropriate opportunities and support, these children accelerate through the initial stages of reading, but some still have problems for other reasons.

Mary, at five years of age, could sort out the most complex system of sets, had the ability to see the essence of a problem, but would not read. Her analytical brain rejected the illogicalities of English spelling and she refused to have anything to do with 'stupid' books. Of course, part of her problem was the realization that here was something she could not do, after five years of being able to grasp most things at lightning speed. A sympathetic teacher and an understanding mother plotted together and mother avoided any mention of reading or books at home. At school, humorous phonic books were introduced to gain the child's confidence, but she only read to the teacher when no one else was around and the entire subject was treated with great secrecy. As her confidence grew, so did her reading ability because soon she had no need to look at words singly, thus avoiding the very illogicalities that caused the original problem. Finally, at an assembly attended by parents, including her mother, the little girl stood up and, for the first time in public, read a complex piece of her own choosing. The child was justifiably proud and the mother and teacher pleased to see her success.

Derek, from a broken home background, transferred at the age of five-and-a-half years from another school which he had been attending since the age of three-and-a-half years. His mathematical ability was excellent and his interest in reference books and stories was insatiable. However, he refused to read because reading was 'boring', and his argument was that if you learned to read, you had to do hard work like his brother and sister, and he did not want to grow up. His older brother and sister were studying for their senior secondary examinations and his parents, although living separately, met regularly but spent the time arguing. Since Derek had to learn to read, however, a new tack was tried. As well as picking out simple books with a high interest or humorous content, each day Derek was given a riddle, which was read to him. He took this home, read it to whoever would listen, and collected ideas for answers. The following day, the answers were read to him and the riddle pages were successively fastened together to make a book, which became part of the class library. *Derek's Riddle Book* became a prize possession and Derek gained prestige because he was the only one who could read the unfamiliar words, and as he read and re-read these, his interest in reading increased.

To supplement the teacher's observations of all the children, we use two objective tests: the British Picture Vocabulary Scale[3] and the Raven's Non-Verbal Coloured Matrices.[4] (The Non-Verbal Raven's Coloured Matrices provides an indication of the child's perceptual adequacy and the British Picture Vocabulary Scale gives an indication of a child's listening vocabulary.) The results of these tests are discussed in the light of the teacher's observation, and anomalies investigated. One such anomaly is revealed in the following case study.

Susan was a very quiet, withdrawn child who always tended to be on the edge of the group, where she fiddled with her socks or someone's hair. Although she produced neat work, the content was hardly remarkable and she contributed little else to school. She scored above the 90th percentile on both tests and consequently her mother was interviewed. Susan had a very bright older sister who was the obvious star of the family, while Susan herself was hardly noticed. Her mother commented that Susan was defiant and argumentative which was in complete contrast to the quiet acquiescent child we knew at school. At two years of age, she had been able to write her name and did so for clinic staff who refused to believe her mother. At home she read constantly and wrote long involved stories spanning many pages which she then read to her school of dolls. She had really enjoyed strategy games, jigsaws and construction toys and, at four years of age, had her own tool kit. Yet this child had been assessed as average by her teacher who was making a conscious effort to assess each child's abilities. After the testing, the teacher deliberately began to elicit detailed responses from Susan, whose non-specific answers only brought a further, more searching question. At first Susan was very hesitant, but her teacher patiently waited for an answer and then praised her every effort. After a month, her mother remarked that she was a different child. Suddenly, someone was listening to her, her opinions were valued and she became a separate person rather than a shadow of her sister.

Whilst any test result must only be taken as an indicator of certain skills and must be considered together with other relevant knowledge, this case study indicates a valuable use of some testing at the mid-infant level.

Relevant and challenging work is essential for a very able child if s/he is not to become disillusioned with school at an early age and working through class or group projects seems to be one answer. While it is essential that the children suggest topics, the teacher obviously also introduces some of her own to extend those of the children and to introduce new ideas. The common problem with topic work is that it only scratches the surface of a subject and is often little more than a rewriting of textbook material whereas, with ingenuity and original thinking, it is possible to make almost any topic relevant and interesting to the children.

How to design projects is outlined on pp. 68ff, but several points need to be reiterated. An infant project should carefully incorporate the basic concepts and skills and must always start from the child's perceptions and the child's knowledge. Supportive reading material is obviously essential and a wide range of reference and fiction will not only satisfy the very able reader but can be used, with help, by the poorer reader. Even when a project is broadly planned, the teacher needs to be sufficiently flexible to capitalize on any opportunity for extension which occurs.

One of our projects, 'Working with Dinosaurs', has already been outlined (on pp. 84–88), but I would like to raise a number of issues which arose as a result of that project.

Teachers had previously been used to working separately on class-based activities without necessarily cooperating and exchanging ideas as a team. After the first team effort, teachers felt stimulated and inspired and commented on their feelings of personal satisfaction. Problems had been openly discussed and shared, a sense of isolation eased.

The basic skills and concepts were not taught separately but incorporated into the project. This meant that teachers had to define clearly what they were doing and why. One teacher was concerned that the children had no specific reading scheme and that she was not hearing children read as often as she would like. Consequently, all the reference and fiction books on dinosaurs were graded for difficulty and then colour-coded. A parents' meeting was held to explain the system. They were asked to help by hearing their children read, marking the reading card and adding any relevant comment. Various strategies for hearing children read were discussed, including the use of word-attack skills, cloze techniques and checking comprehension after silent reading. This was regularly supervised by the teacher who checked and guided both parents' and pupils' progress.

Another early problem which we did not expect was the children's attitude to the 'work'. A class discussion was under way about the colour of dinosaurs, and after 45 minutes of continuous, challenging theory-swapping, a break was called for milk. A very young and bright child asked, 'Aren't we going to do any work this morning?' The children told a stunned teacher that they had not worked because they had not put anything in their books yet. After the break, another discussion was instigated and it was discovered that for many of the children work meant *writing something down*. The ensuing staffroom discussion reflected the fact that this was a serious indictment against us, and a positive approach was needed to change attitudes. Thus, at every opportunity the children's attention was drawn to the importance of *thinking*, and positive attempts were made to convince them that they were working hard when they were thinking.

By carrying this attitude over to the parents, we also eased the problem of those pupils with poor manual control, which is common among very able children. Whilst most children learn to read and write at roughly the same time, very able children may have been able to read for as long as they can remember, or they skip through the initial stages of reading very quickly. By contrast, their writing skills are much slower to develop and the frustration caused by this intensifies the problem. An anxious parent may be placated by the catchphrase 'His brain works faster than his hand', but this does little to help the child who may either be very embarrassed about his/her inability to write legibly, or may even have given up attempting to write and is now unconcerned about it. Both attitudes produce far-reaching consequences because the child cannot express his/her ideas in a written form and may be underestimated as a result. The Dinosaur project set out to cut longhand writing to a minimum and to use mathematical diagrams and charts to record the results of investigations and to help the child to organize his/her thinking. Whilst creative story and poetry writing was prolific, it was possible for the children to express their ideas through cartoons or tape-recordings, with the need for writing cut down to titles and a synopsis of the contents. The important task was to keep the children interested and motivated and to build in writing practice casually without the child being aware of it.

The children's response to the Dinosaur experiment was most rewarding. The zest and verve with which they all worked was beyond our expectation and gave us added impetus to extend the range of the work. The most able did extensive research in depth and breadth and suggested aspects of investigations they would like to pursue. This often continued out of school: one very able child, who had previously been a non-attender but who had not missed one day during the entire term, arrived one morning with a list that he and his friend had collected. This consisted of an analysis of the Latin names of the dinosaurs with the English translations categorized into meanings. This became a standard reference work within the classroom and was most useful when we made our own 'inventasaurs' and needed relevant names. It also helped the more able children with work on syllabification.

Because of the children's obvious interest, parents were most generous in their support and at one point we had more fossils than the local museum, and samples of actual dinosaur bones. A zoologist came to discuss the relationship between dinosaurs and modern animals and was astounded by the children's general knowledge and ability to question him. The staff of the Natural History Museum in London, who took the children on escorted tours around the dinosaur exhibits, were equally astonished by their interest, depth of knowledge and ability to reason.

Although the experiment had been initially provoked by the needs of several very able children, all the children benefited, growing in self-assurance and developing independent working habits. The County Reading Survey, held at the beginning of each summer term, produced results far exceeding those of previous years, thus allaying fears of staff about 'hearing children read'. The dinosaur theme had been chosen because it was an easy and obvious starter for teachers and children, with a wealth of resources available. Not all topics have been so all-embracing, but the general underlying plan of working in this way has produced very interesting projects, such as hatching chickens, keeping mini-beasts, designing our own aeroplanes and redesigning public notices. Almost as important as the effect on children is the reaction of the staff: they realize that extra work is required but they are alert and interested, thinking creatively and they are prepared to innovate, while developing a fuller understanding of basic skills which need to be taught. Although all the children have benefited, perhaps none has benefited more than the few very able children who were just ticking over before but now find school a stimulating and challenging place.

References

[1]CLAY, M. (1976) *Concepts of Print* London: Heinemann Educational

[2]LDA (Learning Development Aids). For a full catalogue of language and skill techniques which are useful for assessment write to LDA, Park Works, Norwich Road, Wisbech, Cambridgeshire PE1 32AX.

[3]BRIMER, S. and DUNN, J. (1962) *British Picture Vocabulary Scale* London: NFER/Nelson

[4]RAVEN, J. C. (1956) *The Non-Verbal Raven's Coloured Progressive Matrices* Sets A, Ab, B Slough: NFER

Appendix D

Developing Cooperation and Independence in a Junior School

John Evans and Sybil Camsey

John Evans is the headmaster of a junior school (pupils aged 7+ to 11+ years), and Sybil Camsey is the deputy headmistress. They believe that pupils should be taught how to learn independently and have devised a special course to encourage the development of study skills. They also promote team teaching so that teachers work cooperatively, sharing ideas and skills. Parents are accepted as cooperative partners, sharing the responsibility for their child's education with the teachers. This kind of organization and teaching style not only allows children to work independently but also makes it easier for children to work at different levels.

The school setting

Barnehurst Junior School was established in 1927 to serve the children of the employees of a local factory. There are many children whose parents attended the school. There is one case where maternal grandparents and both parents have all attended the school. The intake now is mostly from the middle of the social strata and numbers 296 children with 10·6 staff plus the headteacher.

The school aims to develop through cooperation between parents, pupils, teachers and the wider community. A second aim is to develop independent learning, i.e. to equip pupils with the skills of self-management, knowing where to locate necessary information and how to use it. These two aims, when put into practice, enable us to capitalize on other people's expertise, to alleviate the demands on the teacher, to promote understanding amongst parents and, most importantly, to equip a child with the skills and knowledge of how to learn.

Promoting independent learning

The emphasis throughout the school is to promote individual and independent learning alongside cooperative group activities. During the first three years, pupils, for most of their time, are grouped with one teacher, but in the fourth year we have devised a special course which could be called a junior-secondary transition course.

There are three aspects to this course: firstly, the pupils are given greater responsibility in structuring their own schedules of work; secondly, they participate in a specially designed study-skills course so that the first three years of their junior-school training can be crystallized; thirdly, the pupils are taught in a team-teaching situation using three inter-communicating classrooms.

Organization of the fourth-year course
The whole top year is regarded as one class unit, working with three or more teachers. The children are divided into 'Home Base' groups for the purposes of registration and pastoral care. These groups have a cross-section of ability and represent a mixture of previous classes. The children have a desk in which they can keep their belongings, but are unlikely to be working in the same place for more than half of their time.

THE PUPILS' TIMETABLE
Each child has his/her own copy of a complicated timetable and learns to follow it. Only teaching or supervised activity times are specified by us – the remaining periods are used at the child's discretion for completion of set assignments. Once this has been done, the children can use any time left for extension activities, reinforcement or to pursue a topic of their own choice, e.g. extra project work, work on the computer, mathematical or scientific research, logic problems, etc.

At present, 23 periods a week are devoted to 'taught' or 'supervised' activities and 17 periods a week are for individual study and completion of assignments. Each child has a record book containing his/her timetable and s/he is responsible for keeping a personal record of assignments set and completed. Assignments are set on a weekly basis in each subject, and are designed in negotiation with the pupil. This means that the depth and breadth of a project can be varied according to the child's needs, interests and ability.

Homework is encouraged for three reasons:

1 The pressure on timetable allocation necessitates extra work being done at home;
2 Children become accustomed to the discipline of pursuing an interest in their own time and they apply the skills learned in school for independent study;
3 Parents are encouraged to supervise these activities and so are involved in their child's education.

Occasionally, children experience problems in coping with the demands made on them. They may have difficulty organizing their time or find the quantity of work set is too much to complete in one week. These problems usually only occur in the initial stages. If, after two or three weeks, they have not been resolved, a daily report system is operated to provide a crutch. This involves having work checked and signed at regular intervals by the Home Base teacher who is responsible for the pastoral care and overall progress of the children in his/her group. If this approach does not work, then the problem is discussed, firstly with the child to discover if s/he can give a reason and suggest a solution, secondly with the parents, and a compromise is negotiated.

ORGANIZATION OF GROUPS
As well as working on individual assignments, children are involved in many different groups – social and academic – throughout the week.
Ability or academic groups: maths, English, reading.
Mixed-ability or social groups: history, geography, art, PE, study skills, science, creative writing, craft, swimming, music/drama, French studies.
Sizes of groups are also varied – from eight or ten children to the whole year group. Groups are very flexible and a child may be transferred either on his/her own request if s/he is finding work too easy or too difficult, or on the basis of teacher assessment.

Developing study skills
While the development and teaching of study skills is important throughout the school, the course in the fourth year is systematically structured to consolidate those skills. Fig. AD1, pp. 130–1, fully outlines the skills incorporated into the course.

As can be seen from the flow diagram, our study skills scheme is extremely comprehensive. Everything a child could possibly need to equip him/her to become an *independent learner* is included. More important, these skills are *taught* – they are not left to chance. It cannot be assumed that any child, even an exceptionally bright child, will automatically acquire these skills through project work or by some magical, natural process. So we include everything from memory games, observation games, concentration exercises, to notetaking and map drawing, designing, researching and recording an individually-chosen project.

We use a varied approach to our work: formal lessons, activity sheets, games, group activities in which discussion and cooperation are vital, and individual exercises. We use a variety of materials: published books and games, and activity sheets that we have devised ourselves. It would be impossible to itemize every activity, but the following examples illustrate some of them.

Classification
This is an important stage in learning to take notes and use information. Recognizing similarities and differences and developing an ability to record information in table/chart form is essential, as is learning to find the relevant books in the library. All of these skills depend on being able to recognize group characteristics.

Mail order catalogues, school photographs and general-knowledge based assignments provide interesting material. It is vital that opportunity should be given for group cooperation and discussion – children learn more in this way than by individual written assignments, and a 'brainstorming' session afterwards in which groups can compare their method of approach is also necessary.

SOME EXAMPLES
1   Prepare small cards on which names of different groups are written, e.g.

Fruit	*Fish*	*Tree*
pomegranate	plaice	sycamore
pineapple	whiting	beech

A good number to have is six groups of ten, i.e. 60 cards. Each name is written on a separate card and all 60 cards mixed up in an envelope. The children have to decide on the 'group name' and sort the cards into these groups.

Many more complicated variations can be included. One envelope could have six different groups of people, e.g. explorers, sportsmen, writers, inventors, politicians, musicians. Children can be encouraged to sort as many as possible from their own knowledge and to check them afterwards by using reference books. To teach them specific library classification, each card can look like a book and have a book title and contents written on it.

2   A variation on this is to have a set of cards with pictures on, e.g. watches. How can they be grouped? square/round face, digital, Roman numeral, leather/expanding bracelet, alarm/calculator etc. This is a very demanding exercise, particularly when it comes to recording information clearly.

3   A third idea is to make sets of twenty cards, each containing a photograph of a child. The child is then given an identity, together with the following information: name; date of birth; address; brothers/sisters; hobbies; favourite lesson; worst lesson etc. The children can use this information, as well as the visual information contained in the photograph, to sort the set into groups. Again the recording is vital. To test the efficiency of the recording, ask questions which can only be answered by reference to the table/chart drawn up. Has any vital information been omitted?

Following instructions
For following oral, written and diagrammatic instructions, origami diagrams are ideal! Children can also make up their own instructions to give to others.

Use of reference books
Sets of cards are prepared about countries. Each group has a set about

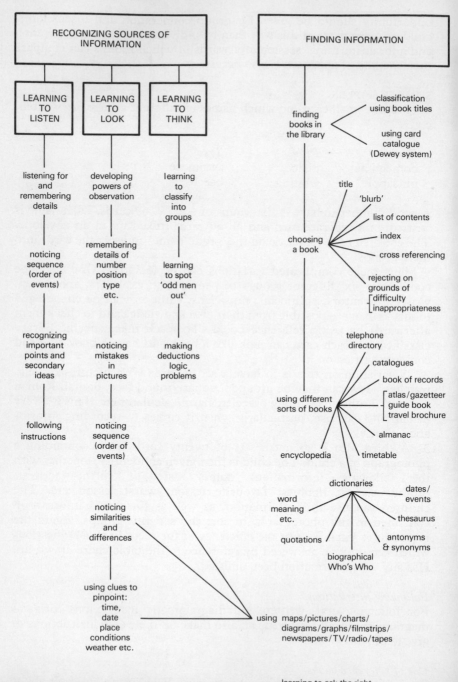

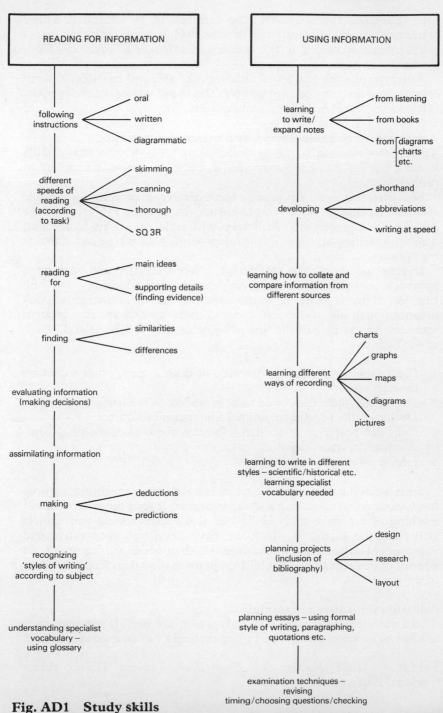

Fig. AD1 Study skills

four countries. One card has map outlines to be identified. Other assignments include identifying famous buildings/places/people, classifying items according to the country of origin, e.g. currency, food, clothes.

This type of work enables *all* children, the able and less able, to work on reference assignments and involves the use of atlases, encyclopedias, dictionaries, travel brochures, almanacs etc.

Applications to project work and other assignments

The work described so far is undertaken separately in study skills lessons, but for it to have any value, it must, of course, be applied to project work.

For two terms in the top year we teach history, geography and science as separate subjects. We do this to ensure that specific subject skills are practised, e.g. specialist vocabulary and style of working, labelling diagrams, writing up experiments, map-work, note-taking and expanding of notes.

During the third term, we adopt a more creative and integrated approach so that all the skills previously acquired can be put into practice. This is done in a mixed-ability group situation so that organizational, discussion and decision-making skills are also brought into use. An example of the sort of topic used is 'Desert Island'. Each group had to:

1 Create their own island – describe it, draw a map, build a contour model;
2 Decide why/how they came to be stranded on the island;
3 Decide on the vegetation, animal life, natural resources;
4 Consider problems of shelter, clothing, food/water/cooking, communication, trade, defence, laws;
5 Decide on a means of escape.

Such work involves a great deal of research, experimenting, testing, discussion, decision-making and organization. It tests the success of our teaching of not only study skills but also organizational and subject skills and the extent to which we have developed cooperative and independent attitudes in our children – both of which are important. As a result of this approach, the children prepare their own final exhibition of work.

Additional resource material

There are some published materials which are useful, although they need to be supplemented. The following books can be used as a basis.

Fergus, A. (1977) *Finding Out From Books* London: Hulton Educational Publications

Jamieson, A. (1980) *Find Out For Yourself* Books 1 and 2 London: Ward Lock Educational

Niven, C. (1980) *Study Skills 1: Finding Information* London: Collins

—— (1980) *Study Skills 2: Reading for Information* London: Collins

—— (1981) *Study Skills 3: Understanding the Information* London: Collins

Team teaching

One of the problems of teaching in a junior school is that we have to teach all subjects, and with the best will in the world we cannot always do justice to them since we all have our own strengths and weaknesses. Within our team-teaching situation, it is not that we have become specialists in certain areas – we *all* teach maths, reading, English, study skills, PE, art and craft – but we have been able to share our ideas and learn from each other. But alongside that we have also been able to develop our own interests in subjects such as history, geography, science, music and French. Through the system we operate, teacher strengths have been developed, weaknesses minimized, and instead of being 'Jacks of all trades' we have, as a team, become 'masters of many'.

One of the advantages of working in a team and of encouraging children to work independently is that eventually the stage is reached where teachers have the time, within the classroom, to help individuals, to prepare new work, to develop new ideas. As the children gain in confidence, self-discipline and independence, they make fewer demands on the teacher. They are able to make decisions for themselves and rarely need reassurance. Consequently, there are times when they are all busy and the teacher is 'redundant'. This time can then be used to great effect working with groups or individuals, making equipment, etc.

Yet another advantage, in a time of economic difficulties, is that resources can be shared. Books and equipment are not needed for three separate classes; instead they are pooled and stored so that they are easily accessible to everyone. With careful planning there is no shortage of books; in fact, a wider variety of books and materials can be provided. For example, instead of having 60 copies of one maths book, three different sets of twenty can be bought. In this way, the children have greater access to a variety of methods, ideas and content.

All work is planned cooperatively and the discussion and sharing of ideas is one of the strengths of the system. Ideas which are partly developed grow and crystallize, planning becomes creative and exciting. But it is not only the teachers who plan in this way; the pupils do too. Involvement in decision-making is a vital part of a child's experience; not only does s/he become independent, but also learns to appreciate the skills and ideas of others.

The leadership and support of the headteacher is essential. In discussions, s/he arbitrates, guides and inspires. It is also important for the headteacher to do as much teaching as possible so that the feeling of team-work and cooperation is enhanced and s/he can also monitor and assess progress.

In the traditional classroom, a teacher is in a very insular position. Ideas and methods of working can become stagnant and the teacher's personal development, over a period of time, can slip into a comfortable format which does not generate inspiration or experiment. Ideas and thoughts may be exchanged in the casual day-to-day conversation of the staffroom, but the time factor does not allow for the expansion of the thoughts at length. When a teacher moves into a team-teaching situation, there has to be a systematic exchange of ideas, agreements on policy and organization, and accepted standards of work and discipline. Education takes on a new dimension as the teacher has to reassess previously accepted standards and methods of teaching.

A major aim of education is to equip a child for living a full and useful life, both as an independent individual and as a member of the community. We try to promote this aim in practice not by talking but by *doing*, by incorporating into our school life the experiences from which a child grows in independence and tolerant understanding of others. We also try to capitalize on the strengths we find in ourselves and in the community and to involve parents as partners in all that we do.

Appendix E

Meeting the Needs of the Individual Within a Large Comprehensive School

David Robinson

David Robinson is Head of the Integrated Studies Unit in a comprehensive school (pupils 11+ to 16+ years of age). He is concerned to develop strategies for identifying the strengths and weaknesses of pupils entering the school so that teachers can more adequately cater for their needs. He is equally concerned to develop team teaching within a flexible organization, devising projects which are cross-curricular and which provide opportunities for pupils to work at a variety of levels according to their abilities.

The Integrated Studies Department at The Appleton School runs a theme-based course for the 330 pupil intake of a twelve-form entry, mixed, urban comprehensive school. The catchment area is largely within a one mile radius from the school, the housing is almost entirely privately owned and employment in the area is mixed, with a large proportion of London commuters.

We suffer from a major pressure in that we are adjacent to a selective area and our potential parents are offered the opportunity of their children competing for places at the grammar schools at eleven plus.

The integrated studies course is designed to develop a balance between meeting individual needs and the development of a truly comprehensive community. Individual differences are deliberately fostered but in a climate of cooperation and each pupil has parity of esteem, whatever their gifts or needs. We insist that the special resources offered to any group, whether the remedial readers or the intellectually gifted, are not developed to the detriment of the remainder.

Integrated studies – an outline of the course
Resources
The facilities available for this course are exceptional but not impossible for other schools to achieve. A partially open-plan unit built to accommodate 180 pupils was opened in 1975 as the final phase in the development of a large comprehensive school campus. The unit has an audio-visual presentation area large enough to seat 120 pupils. This area also houses the closed-circuit television studio, the equipment includes four cameras and it is possible to produce television programmes involving pupils, staff and visitors.

There is a well furnished, enclosed room which is used as a reference and quiet area. Materials available include several hundred books. An uncarpeted area has on-line gas, water and power to enable small-scale science experiments and craft work. The unit also has an office and two storerooms as well as the six class-base areas.

The time allocation is eight periods per week on a 40-period timetable. These are distributed through the week as two doubles and one half-day session. We find the half-day session particularly useful. It allows all pupils to work without the pressure of frequent moves. Of course, most pupils would find it difficult to cope with listening to a lesson or writing quietly for several hours, hence we have developed an approach which involves many changes of activity whilst working on the same theme.

Visits to local museums or environmental visits using the school's mini-buses, listening to an introductory or stimulus lesson, working with small groups of friends, examining slides on the topic, using the school library or the reference room, discussing their work with their class tutor, even working silently on individual assignments are just some of the stratagems organized each session. However, pupils who would find it beneficial to pursue their own study without interruptions have that opportunity and this facility is normally but not always, taken up by the able pupils.

The course materials are devised and produced by the staff team and are supplemented by the resources in the reference room, a slide collection and broadcast materials taped on sound and video. Pupils are also involved in planning projects and building resources. A number of our resource packs have been used by other schools and two have been published by Essex County Council Audio-Visual Resources Department. A pack on the East Coast floods of 1953 includes taped eye-witness reports, newspaper facsimilies, maps, technical information, story extracts and a newsreel film. The second pack, a study of Tilbury Docks, includes maps, technical information, graphs and tables and slide-tape packs on the workings of this important dock complex.

The staff, who are drawn from several subject areas, work as a team in preparing the course materials, presenting lessons, assessments and in allowing flexible groupings of the pupils which is such a fundamental part of our approach. Our normal staff, pupil ratio is 1:25·7 but we have a weekly period with a more generous 1:22·5. However this is just a starting point; the flexibility of our group size is an essential part of the logistics of the course.

Pupil groupings – a flexible approach
The basic group is the form unit, a mixed group of no more than 30 pupils. They are placed in a largely alphabetical arrangement with adjustments made for social reasons and to provide a degree of planned mixed ability on the basis of the primary school evidence. The attempt to balance the mixture of abilities followed pressure from teaching staff

outside the Integrated Studies Department who argued that the mixture of abilities was so random that it made their course organization and deployment of staff difficult.

In the integrated studies situation the actual composition of the form groups proved to be of little consequence. What did prove critical however was having accurate information about the pupils readily available. We discovered that we could not entirely rely on the primary school records. Scores were often missing and many tests of basic skills had been completed several months before the children arrived at the secondary school.

As outlined earlier flexible groupings for a wide variety of activities is an important part of the course. Some of these groups do not require complex assessments: repeat lessons for absentees, working on assignments with small groups of friends and a half-form group using a school mini-bus for a visit are some examples. However, groups such as remedial reading, reinforcement of lessons with groups experiencing difficulties and curriculum extension for very able pupils all require fine assessments.

Any such arrangements are only possible with the full cooperation of the staff team. Staff have to be prepared to take very large groups, 100 + on occasions, but more important, staff have to be flexible enough to disrupt their own timetable and plans at very short notice.

Assessment profiles
The primary school records contain the standardized scores for the NFER (National Foundation for Educational Research) DE Comprehension Test[1] and the raw score for the NFER Mathematics Tests.[2] Between 85 and 90 per cent of these scores are available each year. In those cases without these objective scores a teacher-based score is noted for attainment in mathematics and English. In a small percentage of cases there are no records available.

During the first half-term we administer the NFER DH Non-Verbal Reasoning Test[3] and the standardized score is noted. The correlation between the rank order in the NFER Verbal and Non-Verbal tests is high: 1980 = +0·82, 1981 = +0·87, 1982 = +0·84 (n. approximately 330). When we have noted superior scores on the Non-Verbal test i.e. where the scores are more than fifteen points different then the pupil is interviewed. Experience over three years of testing has led us to the conclusion that a high score (120+ standardized score) on the Non-Verbal test coupled with relatively low scores on Verbal and school attainment tests indicates an under-achiever. Such pupils are closely observed and counselled.

The Richmond Test of Basic Skills[4] is also administered during the first half-term. The standardized scores for the eleven tests involved (English – vocabulary, reading comprehension, spelling, punctuation, use of words and phrases, use of capital letters; maths – concepts, arithmetic; study skills – reading maps, reading graphs and tables, use of reference materials) are noted on the pupil's profile.

The next stage is to simplify all the information so that it can be readily used by the teaching staff.

The school uses a five-point assessment scale based on a normal distribution curve. The standardized scores are converted to this form in order that comparisons with school achievements can be easily made. This table shows how the system operates:

Grades	Standardized scores	Percentage of pupils on normal distribution
1	119+	10
2	109–118	20
3	92–108	40
4	81–91	20
5	−80	10

This information, available by the end of the first half-term, together with pupils' performance and subjective teacher assessment, is used, together with primary school reports, as a basis of discussion on the grouping of pupils for some of their activities. As the teachers learn more about the pupils, and as the pupils reveal their particular strengths and interests, teachers are able to reassess those pupils and respond to their needs.

Many pupils have one or two specific problem areas, such as some aspects of spelling or handwriting. Such specific problems can be noted by the tutor who will guide and note a pupil's progress during the first year. Other pupils exhibit considerable strength (130+ standard points score) in one or two areas but have only average (100 standard points) scores in the remaining tests. Again, these individuals have to be noted by their tutor.

Ideally we would wish to devise individual programmes of work designed to match individual strengths and weakness. However, even with our generous staffing ratio (1:22·5) we are not able to achieve this ideal. We therefore group pupils but use a whole range of tests and observations to do this and we keep the progress of individuals within groups under continual review.

Course aims – a comprehensive approach
The course has a number of aims in the area of the child's social development which are deliberately organized rather than remaining 'hidden' within the curriculum. Integrating intellectual studies to produce learning skills and sound foundations across many subject

areas is important but then so is the integrating of some 330 new pupils into a community of 1,700. Hence any groupings of pupils, for whatever purposes, are not allowed to override the comprehensive community nature of the course. The frequent occasions when assignments have to be completed by friendship groups, plus social events such as discos, lunchtime clubs and excursions, are some of the activities through which community feeling is developed.

The intellectual aims are a matter of discussion within the staff team and their respective departments. Following a team meeting, the specialist staff develop the agreed aim, producing a series of objectives. Once the concepts involved have been examined by the subject specialists then the staff team decide what portion of that concept is considered essential. This portion of the topic is termed *basic work*. All pupils are expected to achieve successful completion of this basic work.

Materials are prepared and collected and a period of time is allocated. The resources of materials and time are planned bearing in mind that all pupils are expected to complete the basic work successfully. Resources can be altered according to staff assessment of how well the pupils are completing their assignments. The basic work materials and lessons have to provide a variety of approaches so that pupils who are experiencing difficulties do not become bored by the necessary repetition.

A second tier of resources is also prepared based on taking the basic concepts further. This *additional work* uses higher order cognitive skills[5] and is designed to provide challenging assignments. All pupils have the additional work assignments available but may only move on from the basic work when their tutor is sure that they have understood the basic concept involved.

Occasionally it becomes obvious that a large number of pupils are experiencing difficulties with the basic work. The strategy which is then adopted is to revise the written materials and to timetable a new series of lessons. The exact nature of the revisions is discussed informally during the actual lesson time and again, more formally, at the weekly staff meeting.

An illustration might make the process clear. We felt that all pupils should be able to use an atlas so that they could find with relative ease the positions of features or places on maps. The geography specialists worked out the detailed objectives. The English specialists examined the written material in terms of readability. The key lesson (introductory lesson to a fresh topic) seemed to go well, and the initial stages of the basic work – finding places on local maps – proved a success. Then things began to fall apart.

Very few of the pupils had really understood the use of coordinates, particularly when based on latitude and longitude. They had been finding local features by their relative positions and not by using coordinates as we had intended. A fresh series of short lessons on coordinates, latitude and longitude were quickly devised by the geographers whilst the rest of the team enlarged the local aspects by introducing Ordnance Survey maps of our immediate area. A short test on the understanding of coordinates was devised and those pupils – in fact a small minority – who indicated that they had mastered that skill moved on to the additional work. The majority of the pupils followed the new lessons which included a considerable number of practical tasks.

The time allocation for this topic had to be extended by three weeks. It was then the responsibility of the geography specialists to convince the team of the worth of the topic in terms of the resources, especially time, given over to it.

Each topic arranged into its components of basic and additional work is designed to allow individuals to make progress at their own speed whenever possible. The introductory *key lesson* and the immediate follow-up discussion with their tutor are two of the few occasions when all pupils in a form group are following the course at the same speed.

For the majority of their time in the Integrated Studies Unit the pupils work at their own pace. However, as I mentioned earlier, we can only approximate towards the ideal of individually-tailored courses. But pupils *need* to work in groups in order to discuss ideas and to learn to work in cooperation with others and we also have to make efficient use of the staff available by arranging some groups. Pupils are differentially grouped for a variety of reasons. The following section describes work carried out by one group of very able children.

Intellectually able group

The pupil profiles are examined and those pupils who achieve almost all grade one results (within the top 10 per cent of the ability range) are discussed at a staff meeting. The tutors' observations of the pupil performance during the first few weeks of term are added to the objective evidence. The pupils are then interviewed and observed at work. The class tutors are asked to pay special attention to any sign that a pupil appears to be under-achieving and any such pupil is interviewed. This is by no means an unusual procedure, since frequent discussions occur between individual teachers and pupils. Also, it is usual to have discussions with parents and over 90 per cent of the parents attend general and consultative meetings.

As explained above, these very able pupils would be expected to be working on the additional work assignments at an early stage in each topic. This group also have a single period each week following a programme on thinking skills, which is largely discussion-based, and a series of lectures which examine the development of our language and literature. The remainder of the year group have their *silence time*, usually silent reading, for 30 minutes during that session. This very able group also have a weekly lunchtime meeting during which an extension scheme is followed.

Expeditions

Since 1978 we have developed an extension programme which is probably unique. The very able pupils have the opportunity to take part in one of three particular expeditions. (Other courses/expeditions are arranged for mixed-ability groups at different times.)

Each expedition involves a full year's preparation, a residential week and a report. All able pupils are expected to take part in the preparation element which is based on the series of archeological detective programmes researched for the BBC by Michael Wood.[6] Each of the nine units deals with one of the great mysteries deep in the roots of our culture. Each subject is dealt with by a close examination of primary source materials and discussions with leading researchers in the area.

The expeditions themselves follow a similar thread of examination of primary sources and discussions with researchers – but this time on site, rather than by observing films. These particular expeditions incorporate greater depth and breadth than most pupils could cope with. Reference books and resources are of a very advanced level, frequently up to university level.

Expedition West is an exploration of the south-west region of England. We begin in Salisbury, journey to Bath, across the moors to Tintagel and Land's End then return with stops at Exeter and Winchester. Each night is spent at a youth hostel and each day includes a tough but exciting mixture of detective work, painstaking observation and recording and physically-demanding exploration of wild moors, fells and remote sites. The theme of this expedition is prehistory and the Roman invasion and settlement.

Having spent Easter basking in the relative warmth of the West Country we move north for the Spring Bank Holiday week. *Expedition North* tours the wild borderland along Hadrian's Wall. Beginning in York we then spend two nights on the wall itself, travel to the western fringes and thence to Keswick and the remote fort at Hardknott Pass. Our last night on this expedition is in the heart of the Pennine Peaks at Castleton. The theme here is the Roman occupation and provincial civilization.

Expedition Cymru is a tour of Wales examining the clash of cultures between the Celtic peoples and their invaders from Roman to Norman times. This summer expedition starts at the Norman castle in St Braivels, moves westwards to Broad Haven then northwards, spending two nights on Snowdon, east to the border city of Chester returning along Offa's Dyke to St Braivels.

The result of the year's work is an illustrated report which includes a large proportion of original research as well as the more usual library research. These reports together with our own expedition reference books and published resources form the basis of an increasingly large collection for the work of subsequent years.[7]

In our view the advantages of the expedition approach to our very able pupils' extension programme are several. Firstly, because this is usually so important in a large secondary school with consequentially large staff political problems, the curriculum is extended without encroaching on an existing subject area. Archaeology uses many of the skills of the Humanities' forms of knowledge together with skills which form part of scientific method but need not infringe on the content of any school subject.

Next, there can be no accusation of cramming the very able pupils in the style of the anachronistic express forms. There is no direct dividend in terms of examination success through following a programme which lies outside the parameters of the traditional curriculum.[8] The experience of exploring primary sources is an exciting approach to opening up young minds to higher-order cognitive skills (such as using evidence to draw conclusions and make judgments). Also the opportunity for sustained effort and achievement allows these children to develop ideas in independent, creative and divergent ways.

Finally, the residential element in the course presents an opportunity for these children to live and work together and to generate and share ideas that could enlighten and enlarge their futures.

References

[1] BARNARD, B. (1974) *Reading Comprehension Test DE* (Standardized Edition) Slough: NFER

[2] (1974) *Mathematics Test DE* (Standardized Edition) Slough: NFER

[3] CALVERT, B. (1974) *Non-Verbal Reasoning Test DH* (Standardized Edition) Slough: NFER

[4] HIERONYMUS, A. N., LINDQUIST, E. F., FRANCE, N. (1975) *Richmond Test of Basic Skills* London: Nelson

[5] After the ideas set out by Benjamin Bloom and his colleagues in the 1960s:
BLOOM, B. S. *et al.* (1965) *Taxonomy of Educational Objectives* Handbooks 1 and 2 Harlow: Longman

[6] WOOD, M. (1981) *In Search of the Dark Ages* London: BBC

[7] We have for example taken many thousands of slides and photographs over the past years. These are used in relevant key lessons for the whole year group.

[8] It should be noted however that this school has experienced increasing success in the examination stakes. Taking the yardstick of 5+ GCE (or equivalent CSE) passes we have moved from 19–26 per cent of our total year group and indications are that this trend is continuing. (GCE: General Certificate of Education – usually taken in the fifth year of secondary education. CSE: Certificate of Secondary Education – a parallel examination.)

Appendix F

Extra Studies: A Form of Curriculum Extension for Exceptionally Able Pupils in a Comprehensive School

Stephen Baines

Stephen Baines has a post of responsibility for Extra Studies in a large comprehensive school (pupils 11+ to 18+ years). Although his aim is to make all teachers aware of the particular needs of the very able pupils in the school, he is able to concentrate on providing extra stimulus for those pupils who need it. His role has many facets: he is a guide, counsellor and facilitator and co-learner with the pupils.

Introduction
'Talent retrieval potency'
Interest in the 'problem' of very able children is not enough. I had been interested in this area for several years, and had read numerous learned works on the subject, which spoke of concepts like 'talent retrieval potency' and 'para-professional teachers', before I realized, in 1977, that my knowledge of the research and my fluency in the jargon was not helping the children in the classroom. It was then that the headmaster and I decided to turn theory into practice and set up 'Extra Studies' at Philip Morant School.

Philip Morant School is a purpose-built 'comprehensive' school in a town that includes two selective schools. It has around 1,300 pupils with a sixth form of some 150. The school is banded in the first three years and setted in the fourth and fifth years. When I first joined the school in the English Department, in 1974, I had assumed that the 11+ examination, however inefficient, must surely identify the most able children; but it soon became clear that it did not, and that we had a number of children of exceptional ability in the school who had 'failed' that test.

Identification
'Very voluble – often at the wrong time'
As a working definition of an exceptionally able pupil, we use: 'An exceptional pupil is one who is outstanding in either potential or achievement in one or more spheres of activity which can be regarded as beneficial to the pupil and to society.' Of course this definition is not exact; nor should it be, since there can be no exact exclusion point for

exceptional ability any more than there can be for shortness, kindness, or foul temper.

With regard to identification, we use a combination of as many methods as are practicable: objective testing, teacher checklists, teacher nomination, self-assessment, parental assessment, and provision itself. For selecting those who will follow the Extra Studies course I am inclusive rather than exclusive, considering all those who have a score in any one test over 130,[1] or who have an interesting disparity of scores. I also pay particular attention to the comments – both spoken and written – of other teachers, for example: 'Quickly sees what she thinks is boring and disrupts accordingly. Always questions rules and requests, etc. Very voluble, often at the wrong time.'

The pupils' words
'Under the relentless pressure of an unseen thumb'
Pupils do tend to understand themselves quite well, and we use a self-assessment questionnaire as one means of identification. But this is a superficial device and it is more useful to listen to what the children have to say – and if we *are prepared to listen*, we shall find that they are often very eager to tell us about themselves.

Apart from conversation, pupils often reveal a great deal about themselves in poetry. A very able second-year boy wrote:

Me, myself, I rarely am
But I hide behind a veil of pretence
I am bombarded with facts and faces
And cower from the vision of the vicious.

Under the relentless pressure of the unseen thumb
I try to crawl to better air,
To take in a clear mind.

I practise my hypocrisies on others
Leading, showing, clowning
They follow, although I fall in my own wake.
I respond to others with a reflective air,
Rebounding their influences.

I am proud to be thought of,
I hold my head up high.
In the ever-deepening, wallowing, mountainous grass of civilization,
I strut.

This, I think, is a good poem, but it is important to remember that mediocre and even poor poetry can be equally revealing. Poems can be useful not merely when the pupil is writing about himself, however, but also as a display – often not made elsewhere – of those qualities that can indicate exceptional abilities, particularly, perhaps, a whimsicality in playing with ideas. Typical is this poem by a fourth-year boy:

Do you know
The world is round but in a
Two-dimensional
Non-Einsteinian
Pseudo-geometrical universe confined to the

$$\sqrt{n\frac{\pi}{x}}\,!$$

Equation, it could, within a byte of the
Imagination
Be flat?
Do you think that they think that
The world is flat but in a
Three-dimensional
Einstenian
Geometrical universe not confined to the

$$\sqrt{n\frac{\pi}{x}}\,!$$

Equation, it could, within a stretch of the
Imagination
Be round?
But . . .

Other forms of writing can also be revealing, such as the essay written by a third-year boy who, when he was asked to describe a scene of his own choice in both winter and summer, chose to write about the bottom of a mine-shaft! Not a way to please one's teacher, but perhaps indicative of creativity.

Another example – and I make no excuse for the plethora of examples since an assemblage of such evidence is an essential complement to formal test scores – comes from a sixth-form girl doing an A level context question on *Troilus and Cressida*. She did the two parts of the set question perfectly then, intrigued by the word 'fraughtage' which appeared in the text, added an additional question of her own – 'Discuss the word "fraughtage"' which she answered as follows:

'Fraughtage! Ah! Here is a word with many layers of allegorical meaning concealed under a cloak of symbolism, and masked with metaphorical associations. I open my dissertation on this noble component of our rich and beautiful language with a brief appreciation of the qualities of sound embodied within it. How strong and vital the word is. What turbulent emotions it creates within even the coldest marbeline breast. One thinks of Persephone with tangled locks shrieking to stormy skies, of Ariadne casting away her broken dreams ...'

It continued in this vein for three more A4 pages, including some splendid suggested derivations for the word, before finishing thus:

I am the only living critic who holds the key to the meaning of 'fraughtage'. But like all good critics I feel it would be unethical of me freely to divulge this valued information!

It is often from such unconventional clues as these that I find I am best able to build up a profile of our most able pupils, and I keep records not only of a child's test scores and checklists, but also of samples of work, essays, poems, cartoons. It sometimes happens that a pupil's best work is what is passed surreptitiously round the classroom on a torn-off corner of paper!

The identification of pupils' abilities is part of a process of coming to know the children as individuals, and consequently it is an ongoing one. However, I make my first selection of pupils for the Extra Studies course during the first half of the summer term of their first year. This normally results in a group of about twelve children, but this group is not fixed, and the pupils may join, or leave or re-join, since flexibility and personal decisions are essential ingredients of the success of Extra Studies.

Teacher antagonism
'Thinks he knows it all'
Provision for exceptional children is an emotive issue, and one that has become entangled with politics and this can raise problems in staffrooms. Also, certain exceptionally able children can elicit antagonistic responses from certain types of teachers – the sort of response a sixth-year boy described in one of his poems:

Childhood extrovert!
Questions everything!
Thinks he knows it all ...

We have tackled this problem by having a staff conference so that issues can be openly discussed. In addition we held a three-day curriculum extension course for exceptionally able children from other schools, and encouraged as many teachers as possible to be involved. A document for staff with guidelines, practical advice and information has also helped to promote understanding and eliminate any initial antagonism there may have been.

The flexibility of Extra Studies, with pupils constantly joining or leaving, also means that those doing Extra Studies are not readily identifiable as a clear-cut group, and this too has helped to reduce any fears people might have had about such provision being 'élitist'.

Purpose and organization
'Her exam results will reflect well on us'
Although the Extra Studies Department has encouraged courses with purely academic content which can lead to better examination results, like the new S level courses, this is not the main purpose of Extra Studies. This needs saying because some teachers and parents tend to regard exceptional children as academic entities which, when prodded, leap prematurely and easily over examination hurdles.

This poem, written by a fifteen-year-old girl in her O level year, expresses the bitterness of someone faced with this attitude:

It is not
how do I feel?
Is this
important to me?

No questions asked.
It is only:
She is
property.

It is not
do I think?
Have I feelings
at all?

Only there is a
brain in there
somewhere.
Plain academic.

It is not
help me,
help me
to be happy.

It is only:
her exam results will
reflect well on us.

A primary need of exceptionally able children, as much as of any other children, is to be valued and accepted for themselves. Their 'self-image' is often surprisingly low and consequently one of the functions of Extra Studies is to provide a vehicle for counselling.

In the second half of the summer term of their first year, pupils are withdrawn from their classes for two periods each week. The time varies so that pupils do not miss the same lessons each week and group projects are undertaken. The summer term is convenient since O and A level examinations are finished and there is greater flexibility of timetabling and less pressure on teaching staff. For second-year pupils I structure weekly lunchtime periods with occasional release from classes particularly for individual pupils, and the emphasis is on individual assignments of personal preference. Third-year pupils participate in lunchtime sessions only, with special project days towards the end of the summer term. Although no Extra Studies had been planned for fourth-year pupils, at their request, projects are continued in their spare time.

Content: group work
'Entirely individual lines'
Projects are essentially *cross-curricular* and *skills-based*. Problems which require convergent thinking are used as well as problems which require very divergent, creative thinking. Problems of code-breaking, and those involving logical, sequential reasoning are tackled. For example, the Language Decipherment project involves comparing a passage of prose written in several languages (French, German, Italian, Latin, Greek) and deducing the rules of syntax and the vocabulary. Pupils also work out how to play chess from Caxton's fifteenth-century account 'The Game and Playe of Chess'.

Creative thinking exercises are used (similar to those of Edward de Bono's work on lateral thinking). Some of the divergent problem-solving involves technological challenges, such as devising a timing device for lessons which will not cost more than fifty pence.

A favourite introductory lesson with first-year pupils poses such problems as: Which is (are) the odd one(s) out: Bat, Owl, Pig, Cow, Horse? Their first assumption invariably is that there is one 'right' answer but when they realize that any one or pair of items can be the odd one(s) out, for a variety of reasons, there is a visible sense of relief and ideas then come quickly. There is almost a sense of being set free.

Thinking skills
This involves a variety of skills from the logical and syllogistic (e.g. 'If nothing that is not a mome rath outgrabes, and some slithy toves outgrabe, then what connection can you deduce between mome raths and slithy toves?') to the brainstorming exercises where as many solutions as possible are imagined (e.g. 'How many uses can you think of for a pair of braces?' and 'How many ways can you think of to improve tourism in Coggeshall?'). In addition to this the pupils practise collecting and evaluating evidence, separating *what* is said from *how* it is presented, in order to come to a reasoned judgment. To do this involves

a certain amount of linguistic analysis, for example thinking about the differences between the sorts of statements being made in the following cases: 'This dog exists', 'Dogs exist', 'Mammals exist', 'I exist', 'God exists'. It also requires the examination of the underlying value judgments and assumptions embedded in such statements as 'Murder is wrong because it's against the laws of God', or 'Abortion is wrong because at eight weeks old the foetus already looks human'. It is often difficult at first to make pupils realize in these last two cases that one wishes to examine the nature of the statements, and not to discuss the topics of murder and abortion – but once this difficulty is overcome, the insights that are shown can be surprising. One can then go on to look at tendentiousness in, say, the writing of history, or physics.

Study skills
It is essential for pupils who will have to cover large areas of information, for study or research to learn the skills of finding, interpreting, assimilating, condensing, organizing, using and recording this information. To this end in Extra Studies we cover a variety of such skills, which includes information-extraction, book-analysis, increasing reading speed, note-taking and note-making and vocabulary enlargement. All this is fairly standard, and there are numerous books on this topic. In the future, as study skills hopefully become part of the regular curriculum for everyone,[2] I envisage this part of Extra Studies being reduced, though not eliminated.

Extension projects
The real culmination of the Extra Studies course is the extension projects, in which all these skills are employed in a long-term project which covers a topic not dealt with in the classroom.

Such a project could be something like our group research into 'Tourism and Tourist Potential in Coggeshall' – the results of which were collated into a full, interesting and useful document.

Most workschemes are devised for individual use. 'The Manor of Wodensfeld'* is such a project, where one is required to run a fourteenth-century medieval estate for a number of years, given details of livestock, farming practices, acreage etc. Each year plans must be made for the following year, then one is given yields and prices (all based on real figures), from which the annual profit is then calculated and plans are made for the next year. The idea is to make the farm profitable.

There is also a companion project which is about a peasant on the same estate who must survive with his/her family. Pupils can then go on to find out about, or discuss, any topics arising, such as how medieval calculations were actually worked out, comparing a medieval diet to a modern one, or considering the history of social injustices.

This sort of project, involving sustained and difficult work, individual decision-making, manipulation of multiple variables, and a great variety of demanding problems – including moral ones – is exactly what exceptionally able children require.

One pupil after tackling 'The Manor of Wodensfeld' wrote: 'Unlike much of secondary school study, we developed this project on entirely individual lines, and by this means it was difficult not to become completely immersed'; another that it was 'the most enjoyable project/game I have ever partaken in' and that it 'was so enjoyable that for a week it was all that I did ... I loved every single minute of it'. And this from children who, if bored, do not hesitate to let you know!

Content: individual provision
'Full stops and capital letters not clearly written'
In addition to, and complementary to, our group provision is a flexible system of individual provision because, although all very able children have certain needs in common, they also have specific personal requirements.

From the second year I see pupils for individual sessions encouraging them to work on interests of their own, developing, challenging and deepening their ideas. This has resulted in work as varied as learning air navigation techniques, analysing historical mortality figures, learning Latin and doing a comparative sociological study on behaviour modification.

There are many advantages of this individual provision. Firstly, it means that I can get to know the children better, and often discover interests and skills that are hidden in the normal run of school activities. Secondly, it encourages pupils to talk; it is unfortunate that many schools tend to train their most able to be good listeners, but poor talkers – and this verbal reticence is a real barrier to developing their own thoughts. Thirdly, and perhaps most importantly, such sessions can be times when a pupil can have a one-to-one education with an interested teacher unencumbered with that battery of concerns such as the proper wearing of uniform, the spelling and neatness of written work and the restrictions of following an examination syllabus. This temporary freedom from these constraints can be invaluable for the 'non-achiever' who has built up anti-school attitudes which hinder his/her true development. It can also be vital for the fostering of creativity in pupils.

Creative thinking is often neglected in schools. What passes, for example, as creative writing in English is often merely formula work, guided and conditioned for examination purposes, by a teacher who adopts a rather negatively critical stance. Such an attitude is illustrated by the written comments on the English work of a very able pupil which are quoted in the *Aspects of Secondary Education*: 'Not thought out ... full stops and capital letters not clearly written ... needs more careful thought ... not developed .... Is this all? ... weak ... poorly expressed

... meaningless ... rubbish.'[3] All this tends to produce a cringing conformity which is merely an undigested assimilation of the results of other people's creativity. True creativity must be fostered in a more positive and 'permissive' atmosphere which accepts and builds on new and half-formed ideas. We must encourage true creativity even at the risk of upsetting the traditionalists, for creativity will often reveal itself – especially in more able children – as satire.

Of course a concern for creativity must involve all departments of a school, but in the Extra Studies Department we can, perhaps, make a special kind of contribution. The virtue of the Extra Studies is that it can respond in a way that is more difficult in the formal classroom, since it can almost privately encourage each pupil's own interest and potential.

Conclusion
'Has engaged his interest'
The whole purpose of Extra Studies is to try to assess and cater for the individual needs of each child.

This might involve a number of things such as putting a pupil in touch with certain people, organizations or courses outside the school, or persuading other members of staff to give lectures, information or sympathy. A pupil may need remedial help with handwriting, or may need counselling; or a pupil with a sporting or musical gift may need help to arrange his academic work so it does not suffer from his periodic absences for training or competitions. The needs of the exceptional child are various, and a school's response must be flexible.

It is difficult to evaluate the work of the Extra Studies Department, since one cannot point to examination passes or other objective criteria. The voluntary nature of Extra Studies makes one painfully aware of the failures – those who opt out and do not respond. But most stay, and some join, and those who are involved find it enjoyable and stimulating. The following extract is from a letter written by a parent of a very able but under-achieving child:

> I know you have had problems with my son this last year, and I thank you for your forbearance. The Extra Studies program has engaged his interest more than anything he has done for some time.

References
[1]THORNDIKE and HAGAN (1978) *Cognitive Abilities Test* London: Nelson
CALVERT B. (1974) *Non-Verbal Test DH* Slough: NFER
Moray House Verbal Test
[2]DES (1975) *A Language for Life* (The Bullock Report) London: HMSO
[3]DES (1979) *Aspects of Secondary Education* London: HMSO
*See p. 90 for further reference to this project.

Appendix G

The Problems of Identifying Under-achieving Pupils in an Urban Comprehensive School

Roger Street

Roger Street is the headmaster of a large comprehensive school (pupils 11+ to 16+ years of age). He is very aware of the deprivation experienced by many of his pupils and wants to develop a caring and supportive atmosphere in the school. He is equally aware that many pupils under-achieve and is keen to provide his pupils with educational opportunities which are relevant and stimulating so that they will be motivated to learn and use their abilities.

The purpose of this appendix is basically threefold:

1 to illustrate the problem of 'bright pupils' under-achieving in school,
2 to record a particular school's response to this problem,
3 to profile a number of pupils' progress through the system.

If there is one thing we are aware of, it is that we are not achieving the level of success we would like. The purpose of sharing our experience is to help highlight the problem and to show by example some of the things that can be done, and some of the things that should not be done!

Westlake Comprehensive

Westlake is a seven/eight-form entry comprehensive school in a new town. It was opened approximately twenty years ago and is a purpose-built school on a fifteen acre site. The catchment area consists largely of densely-packed council housing with four relatively small owner-occupier estates on the periphery.

The majority of pupils are second generation inhabitants of the town and the vast majority come from homes where the father, if there is one, is in a skilled or unskilled manual job, again if there is one. Family break-up is common, unemployment levels are significant, poverty not unknown and commitment to long-term educational objectives is weak.

In 1978 Westlake admitted 203 pupils: 155 from the catchment area (76·4 per cent); 48 from outside the catchment area (23·6 per cent). Of this 203, approximately 81 per cent came from council housing. By 1982 the proportion from outside the catchment area had risen: of the intake of 238, 131 came from the catchment area (55 per cent); 107 from outside the catchment area (45 per cent). Nevertheless, the proportion of pupils from council housing had remained basically the same: in 1978 it was 81 per cent; in 1982 it was 79 per cent.

The majority of pupils when admitted had already been tested in their primary schools, both for a VRQ (Verbal Reasoning Quotient) and a NVRQ (Non-Verbal Reasoning Quotient). There was no uniformity in these tests and in some cases schools outside the catchment area did not forward a score. In 1978 167 pupils had both scores; 4 had a VRQ only; 32 had no score at all. However, in comparing the VRQS and NVRQS, and allowing for the disparity between the tests used, there was a clear indication that, overall, pupils had a lower verbal reasoning score in comparison with their non-verbal reasoning score (see Fig. AG1 below). Since school-based success, in terms of examination success and career opportunity, is highly correlated with verbal reasoning scores, we were concerned that, in general, pupils were under-achieving. We realize

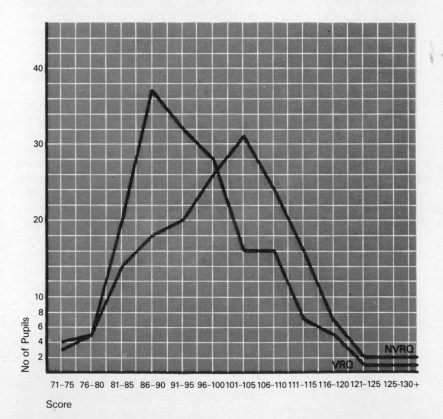

Fig. AG1 1978 intake: NVRQ and VRQ scores based on primary school records

that group tests only indicate certain aspects of a child's ability and performance, but use them as one kind of assessment.

Subsequent testing over several year-groups has revealed a similar pattern of scores. However, a number of pupils showed discrepancies between verbal and non-verbal scores of more than fifteen points, a significant difference, and so a small working party was set up to examine the problem further.

The working party
This group was established in January 1979, under the chairmanship of a senior teacher whose responsibilities included the running of our maths department. The group began by circulating this memo to all staff:

HELP!!!
A small working party consisting of Jo H., Dave M., Colin S., Gordon E., and Helen S-S. has been set up to investigate the provision made for bright children in the school, and to suggest possible improvements.

To this end we have set up a modest survey, to run for a fortnight to monitor the work of twelve pupils. (Here they were named.)

If you teach one (or more) of these pupils, we would like your help in the following way. Every morning during this fortnight a short questionnaire will appear in the lockers of those staff who teach the twelve pupils that day. When you have completed the particular lesson in question, could you please fill in the questionnaire and put it in my locker; it should only take a couple of minutes. Any member of the working party will be glad to elucidate any difficulties with the questionnaire. The pupils will themselves be filling in a questionnaire in their lessons over the fortnight.

I would like to emphasize the following three points:

1 We would like the lessons to be as 'normal' as possible, with no special efforts made with regard to the pupil in question.
2 No value judgments are being made about your particular lesson, so please be honest.
3 Even with only a small-scale survey like this I shall be dealing with over 1,000 pieces of paper. It would help me *enormously* if completed questionnaires could be in my locker by *4.00 pm on the day in question*.

Thank you in anticipation of your assistance.

The teacher questionnaire was as follows

Staff questionnaire

Pupil   Staff   Subject   Day
Period

Please tick as appropriate
1   Arrangement of class   *set   mixed-ability*
2   Brief description of lesson (e.g. discussion and worksheet)
3   Was X busy during   *all   most   some   none*   of the lesson?
4   Did you make any special provision for X during the lesson, or was he doing the same work as the others?   *extra   of the same   different   same as others*
5   Did the lesson depend on mainly factual and routine thought processes or did it demand higher level skills, e.g. abstract thought, analytical reasoning etc?   *mainly routine   higher level*
6   Do   you   think   that   X   found   the lesson   *dull   average   stimulating*   ?
7   Have any factors limited your efforts to extend X? (You may tick more than one.)   *numbers in class   low ability children in class   disruptive children in class   lack of motivation of X   other*

Questions 8 and 9 are on homework set during the lesson. Answer if applicable.
8   Was the homework   *highly structured   some room for X to expand on the minimum   totally open-ended?*
9   How long would you expect it to take X?   *less than 15 mins   15–30 mins   30–45 mins   45–60 mins   over 1 hour*
10 Any comments you would like to make?

Pupils were required to complete two types of questionnaire, one for classwork and one for homework.

Pupil questionnaire: classwork

Pupil   Staff   Subject   Day
Period

Please tick as appropriate
1   Were you fully involved and interested in the work   *all   most - part   none*   of the time?
2   In any discussion part of the lesson, did you feel free to express your own ideas, or were you (or are you ever) inhibited by what other pupils might think?   *a lot   sometimes   never*

3 Did the contribution other pupils made to the lesson help you to learn or understand *a lot   to a certain extent   not at all* ?

4 Did the pace of the lesson suit you or would you have preferred to go *slower   as it was   faster   much faster* ?

Pupil questionnaire: homework

Pupil	Staff	Subject	Day

Period

Please tick as appropriate

1 Time spent on homework *less than 15 mins   15–30 mins   30–45 mins   45–60 mins   over 1 hour*

2 Did you find your homework *interesting   average   dull* ?

3 Did (or might) this homework stimulate you to any further activities related to school work, e.g. reading, discussing with parents, finding out further information? *yes   possibly   no*

Not only did the working group analyse over 1,000 completed questionnaires, they also spent some time talking with the pupils involved in the exercise. Their findings were not encouraging:

1 There was a preponderance of routine, as opposed to higher, skills.
2 Few pupils found lessons stimulating.
3 There was little open-ended homework.
4 Homework seldom stimulated further study.
5 The pace of lessons was often too slow.
6 There was evidence of peer-group pressure not to appear bright.

The report then went on to give some advice on how to identify and cater for bright youngsters. As this part of the report was couched in rather speculative terms, I produced an addendum designed to crystallize some of the positive and practical suggestions arising from the report. Departments were required to discuss both the report and the addendum. The recommendations were as follows.

Recommendations
DEPARTMENTAL
1 Departments will regularly meet to discuss the work of *all* children. At these meetings particular regard is to be paid to the work of the able children. Heads of Department must satisfy themselves that adequate provision is being made for the more able pupils in terms of quality of both classwork and homework. The departmental meeting is the ideal forum in which to discuss problems, share ideas, induct new teachers,

and so on. It is also the ideal place in which to evaluate the effectiveness of ideas outlined below.

2 Staff must keep an accurate record of the progress of all their pupils to try to ensure that youngsters are realizing their potential. Reference must be made to the level of a pupil's ability as measured prior to their coming to Westlake. Sufficient information is available from Heads of House to ensure a fair degree of awareness of each pupil's ability. If we teach youngsters without knowing their capabilities many able children will escape with offerings that are second best.

3 Departments must evaluate the success or otherwise of their teaching strategies. A more individualized approach is both practicable and possible, and a more effective use of our Resource Centre must be developed in order to prepare materials to challenge our able pupils. Again, the departmental meeting is a good place to compare approaches, share ideas on resources, and develop new techniques.

4 Departments must look much more closely at the criteria they use for setting. There is some evidence to suggest that our present system favours the quiet, neat, conforming child, and a number of more difficult but potentially more able pupils find themselves in lower sets. This merely compounds the problem. Ineffective setting creates considerable disciplinary problems.

5 Heads of Department must monitor the performance of the able pupils. This will involve looking regularly at exercise books, inspecting resource material, talking to staff and, hopefully, establishing a 'club' for their subject in which bright youngsters can develop their abilities.

6 Departments must ensure that homework is set regularly and that it is of sufficient quality to demand a significant amount of time and attention on the part of the able child.

We must seek to establish an academic ethos in which the bright child can flourish without fear and/or embarrassment. It almost goes without saying that only in a structured and controlled situation, both in the classroom and outside, can our bright children feel secure enough for their abilities to develop. As a school we have a reputation second to none in remedial and pastoral care. The same care and attention must be given to all our pupils, not least those at the top of the ability range.

CENTRAL

1 A programme of curriculum extension is to continue under the leadership of John R. This programme will continue to develop in an attempt to provide for the very able.

2 A programme of central monitoring of able children is to be investigated.

3 Form prizes for academic attainment are to be introduced next year. These will probably be for all years and are to be awarded at our annual prizegiving.

One of our main objectives had been achieved. We had made the staff aware of the problem and we had begun to encourage departments to develop strategies for meeting the needs of the most able. Although we had a programme of curriculum extension in operation for the academic year 1978/9, we felt that this was no substitute for teaching staff organizing their content and methodology to ensure that able pupils were challenged intellectually.

The curriculum extension programme has continued, and basically consists of an all-age group of pupils meeting with a teacher on a regular basis to follow through an extra-curricular programme on a subject which was designed to foster ongoing activity. For example in 1980/1 we offered four modules: electronics; computing; geology; the Stock Exchange.

It is difficult to say how successful these efforts have been, although there has been a noticeable improvement in the school's examination results at GCE O and A level. What the programme has failed to do is to involve the 'intelligent delinquent' element. Such pupils display two characteristics on entry to Westlake: a significant disparity between VRQ and NVRQ scores; a lack of commitment to education.

We have a significant number of these pupils (about seven or eight in our 1978 intake) and in general their backgrounds are characterized by: language deprivation; family traumas; restricted cultural experience; lack of specific educational input after primary level; poor self-image; inadequate personal relationships; 'discipline' problems at primary school.

In order to meet the needs of these pupils we have sought to develop the specific strategies listed below.

Specific provision for very able children

1 A senior teacher has specific responsibility for able pupils. His role is to:
   chair a think-tank of staff to generate ideas and action to meet these pupils' needs;
   coordinate provision;
   identify very able pupils;
   disseminate ideas;
   keep abreast of 'the subject';
   monitor the progress of our most able children.
2 Our Reading Centre (formerly Remedial Department) caters for all pupils with a learning problem regardless of their ability. The department is a source of expertise and experience on overcoming the reading/writing problems sometimes experienced by the most able. It is also a fertile source of imaginative ideas for ongoing work.
3 The needs of the most able pupils is a subject dealt with under our programme of in-service education. This is designed to: educate the staff; initiate discussion; foster ideas; stimulate action. As a result of

this the needs of the most able have become an element in a Head of Department's accountability discussion with the Head.

4 The attention of the Governing Body has been drawn to the work of the school with these pupils and is an element in the Governors' programme of curriculum review.

We do have the feeling that we are merely scratching the surface with our specific provision, but it is at least a base on which to build, and there are positive outcomes. The English Department in response to our in-service education is organizing a workshop weekend for all our most able pupils and we hope to extend this enthusiasm and commitment across the subject boundaries.

General provision

By this I mean overall developments in the school which are designed to benefit all our pupils, although they are undertaken in the awareness that they will be of particular benefit to the most able.

1 We have actively sought to develop our curriculum away from the chalk/talk/factual recall syndrome, and to concentrate on pupil involvement and the development of skills.

Progress is patchy, but there have been some genuine improvements:

a new pupil-centred integrated science course in Years 1 and 2;
a new task-centred geography course in Year 1;
a programme of study/learning/reading/writing skills in Years 4 and 5;
new history resources in Years 1 and 2;
the establishment of a library/exhibition centre;
the development of the library as a resource centre.

Innovative work is often the result of the efforts of a single teacher and it is essential for schools to seek to appoint staff who are aware of the needs of 'bright' children; have imagination and creative ability; are willing to commit themselves to the development of resources to meet the needs of these pupils.

It is interesting to note that in one of the profiles that follows, an art teacher of outstanding creative and imaginative ability played a crucial part in the development of an under-achieving pupil.

Extra-curricular activities are crucial. Clubs which demand a high level of intellectual/imaginative commitment can help very able pupils enormously. There is tremendous scope in areas such as chess, computers, drama, art, pottery, electronics, design, war games, and frequently a commitment to and success in a 'non-academic' subject will bring about an improvement right across the board.

2 A clear policy on homework is essential. Homework should be

stimulating and challenging, imaginative and open-ended; an opportunity for pupils to show us what they are capable of when left to themselves with perhaps nothing more than guidelines. Much homework reflects teaching which is dull and unimaginative. Our Senior Teacher, who is responsible for able pupils, also monitors our homework programme.

3   The staff meet regularly to discuss pupils and to share experiences and ideas. My failure might be somebody's success and they can share their ideas and strategies of success with individual pupils.

4   We have given a lot of attention to the 'hidden' curriculum. We have consciously tried to remove fear from the school and to a large extent have been successful. This helps bright pupils to feel at ease and to be willing to stand out as different. Our next major target is to remove 'boredom'.

We have sought to generate a feeling of mutual respect for each other, regardless of our individual aptitudes or differences. If pupils can feel comfortable in school they will begin to grow. Is it too much to ask that they be happy too?

Having said all that, we still feel that there is so much more to be done, so much more effort to be put into: improving the curriculum, developing resources, improving the environment, establishing a healthy ethos, training staff.

I have tried to give some idea of how we are beginning to meet the challenge, and a challenge it is. Here are five very bright pupils and the history of their first four years at Westlake. I suggest you make your own assessment, judgment, evaluation – I wish simply to record the facts.[1]

Case studies[1]

Kate

Age on entry	11 years 10 months
VRQ	107
NVRQ	127
Father	Warehouseman, not living with the family.
Mother	Works at a distillery all night to support the family.
Siblings	Three – two already in Westlake, one to come.

Primary report
Kate is a pleasant hardworking little girl. She is a bookworm. .... Her mathematics concepts are clear and precise. She can swim and joins in country dancing. She is a member of Guides.

Within a few months of joining Westlake Kate was having problems:

poor attendance, absences often covered by a note from mother,
very poor punctuality when in attendance,
little homework produced,
friendless,
extremely quiet and uncommunicative,
very little confidence.

Kate's first-year subject reports were, not surprisingly, very poor, the general comment being that she was undoubtedly a very able girl but was under-achieving. Her second year report was even worse although staff were noting her ability to 'over perform' in examinations considering how little work she did.

During her second year she was seen by an educational psychologist who reported:

I saw Kate on November 11, but she refused to take any tests. She was very offhand, defensive, and resistant. I got the impression that she was a depressed child under the veneer of disinterest. She admitted that she had no friends, said that she was used to the situation and it wasn't a problem.

Kate was subsequently referred to a child guidance clinic who felt that with support and encouragement, her commitment to study would improve. This proved to be the case.

Early in her fourth year Kate's attitude changed and by the fifth year she was committed to a programme of O levels in English language, English literature, maths, physics, computer studies, history, with French and typing CSE. Her fourth-year report was characterized by A grades for both effort and attainment.

We feel this improvement has been brought about by a number of factors:

1   Kate's tutor, a highly gifted art teacher, managed to get Kate involved in a major art project. This was a significant breakthrough and produced an immediate improvement in Kate's attendance, punctuality, and demeanour.
2   Kate's mother stopped working at night and began to take more interest in her, producing a greater stability and sense of security at home.
3   Kate began to make new friends in her O level sets and to discuss her work with them. She enjoyed the security of being with pupils of similar ability.
4   We made Kate a prefect to capitalize on these developments and this provided a further boost to her confidence.

Kate is now committed to taking A levels with the probability of a career in engineering. She is in the school play – *Macbeth*. There are still problems at home with study facilities and we are encouraging her to study in school at the end of the day. We are confident that Kate will continue to make good progress.

Mark

Age on entry	11 years 2 months
VRQ	99
NVRQ	123
Father	Redundant.
Mother	Assistant at a playgroup.
Siblings	Two older brothers, one recently deceased.

Primary report

Mark's written work is appalling mainly because he is just not interested in learning anything concerning this aspect of academic work. However, almost the opposite can be said of this so far as maths is concerned. His mother finds it hard to accept his inability to do well in English. Not an endearing person or personality. ... Mother cannot accept Mark is not very clever.

Mark's first-year secondary report contained the following comments:

Maths	Mark is in the top set and has a sound understanding of the subject. His work suffers from poor presentation.
Science	Mark is very interested in practical work and has excelled in tests. His written work, however, is very weak.
Reading Centre	... a spelling problem in an intelligent boy such as Mark can cause great confusion and distress, it is to Mark's credit that he attempts to deal with it so sensibly and reasonably ... he is creative and has very good ideas ... Mark needs to begin to take responsibility for his own actions and to be less reliant on the limits set by adults ... he is a pleasure to teach.

Mark's mother took him to their local GP who subsequently requested information from the school as his mother 'has informed me that Mark suffers from significant learning difficulties and is a suspected case of dyslexia'. In the reply to the doctor we said:

Mark is a well-motivated boy who is anxious to please and works hard to keep up in class. He arrived at Westlake with a poor record of achievement at primary school, and with a report indicating that he was lazy and uncooperative. We have never found this to be so in his work at secondary level; but his progress has been hampered by his difficulties with reading and he does not find it easy to concentrate on reading or to find his way unsupported through a text. He received special remedial help in reading and writing in his first year.

In his second year, however, he has returned to mixed-ability classes in all subjects and although there is no doubt that his progress is slow because he finds reading and spelling difficult he is determined to succeed and has shown considerable effort in all aspects of his work. In maths and science he works with a top set and is able to use his considerable intelligence with more ease. Mark is thoughtful and intelligent in his approach to school, liking to talk and discuss, and is very interested in things around him.

He is often anxious because of his feelings of inadequacy over his spelling and reading problems, and this anxiety is no doubt increased by the fact that his mother is very anxious about his progress and worried about defending Mark from the charge of laziness and lack of effort. His father is not convinced that his spelling difficulties are real and I think that an outside agency giving some kind of objective assessment may well ease the tension – this in itself would help Mark to approach his difficulties with more equanimity and less anxiety.

Nothing came of this initiative but the school was fortunate enough to be able to give Mark private access to a clinical psychologist who produced a set of guidelines for us.

SUGGESTED AIDS TO ACADEMIC SUCCESS FOR MARK
1   Ensure Mark is taught: essay writing skills; study techniques; organization of notes for revision; advanced and effort-saving reading skills.
2   Ensure he understands and has practice in responding to the various examination terms commonly used and the various forms of multiple-choice questions (some of which may be very complicated).
3   Ensure he collects adequate notes on class work by:
   using a tape-recorder during relevant parts of lessons;
   learning note-taking techniques;
   developing a personal shorthand. (This could be developed by Mark working out his own symbols or shortened forms for commonly occurring terms listed by his various subject teachers.)
4   Provide him whenever possible with textbooks or worksheets which cover the work done in class so that he has adequate material to study and for revision.
5   Continue to allow him aids with multiplication since he does not have a firm knowledge of multiplication tables (a common occurrence in

children with specific learning difficulties of this type).

6 If Mark needs to do homework at school rather than at home this opportunity should continue to be provided.

Expect and insist that he does his homework (unless there are good reasons why he cannot).

Where possible and practical allow him more time than usual to complete his homework.

Ensure that he understands why he loses marks on homework and in exam work when this occurs (so that he knows how he needs to improve).

7 Ensure that Mark understands what exam qualifications are required for the careers which interest him and that he understands the level of work required from him now in order to obtain the necessary qualifications.

8 Understand that Mark's verbal reasoning ability and verbal understanding are well above the average, while his reasoning in the non-verbal area is outstandingly high. Thus expect work from him the content of which shows understanding and reasoning at such levels, even though the work may be marred by, for example, untidiness, poor writing, poor spelling, poor expression of ideas, misunderstandings when complicated passages are required to be read or when the work relies on note-taking. (Mark's notes might be inadequate or inaccurate; at present it appears that he mainly relies on his memory.)

9 Expect that Mark, with help and understanding from those around him, will be able to find ways around his difficulties if he is sufficiently well motivated to do so.

10 Discuss with Mark any puzzling aspects of his performance; although he is not good at expressing his ideas either in conversation or in writing, he has good understanding of his difficulties.

11 Mark probably does not have a clear understanding of his own abilities nor clear expectations of himself (which is understandable since those around him have had very varying expectations of how he will perform and achieve). His confidence in himself is shaky and he needs help in achieving a realistic view of himself.

Progress with Mark is still limited. His latest report contains the following comments:

Maths (O level group)	Mark shows every sign of being able to understand the concepts involved at O level, but being unable to understand the exam requirements and techniques due to his language problems. He is always punctual, works well unless he finds real difficulties with the questions. Encouraging progress has been made.
English (O level group)	*Attainment* Mark's English is full of spelling mistakes but slow progress is being made, especially in

the area of self-correction. His scripts, however, tend to be short.

Potential At times has shown real creative potential.

Attitude Positive, much improved on last year's attitude.

Relationships Tends to sit alone, little patience with fools.

Summary Mark is making pleasing progress and beginning to show a quiet self-confidence. The progress, however, is slow, and he still has a long hard climb to success at O level.

Physics (O level group)	Needs constant encouragement to reach a satisfactory standard. Definite O level ability.
Chemistry (O level group)	Has demonstrated a good level of attainment. Enthusiastic and hard working.

Peter

Age on entry	11 years 6 months
VRQ	105
NVRQ	127
Father	Chargehand electrician (not living at home).
Mother	Part-time shop assistant.
Siblings	Two older brothers.

Primary report:
A brilliant gymnast, enjoys games. Aggressive to other children.

First-year secondary report

Science	Attainment A mixed ability	Test results consistently good, written work of a high standard but untidy, occasionally a bit silly in class. Practical work good.
Maths	Attainment A Set 1 or 5	A talented mathematician, he grasps new topics readily ... capable of good work in the more abstract parts of the subject. It is unfortunate that Peter's work is always so untidy.
English	Attainment C mixed ability	Peter tries hard and is anxious to succeed but his attainment is limited because his reading age is below average, and his English lacks the style and grammatical correctness that constant readers are beginning to possess. He is more than able to answer questions correctly in class so his difficulties do not stem from lack of understanding.

Peter's subsequent history was one of deteriorating attitude and behaviour: truancy, vandalism both on the school site and in the community; disruption of lessons; unpunctuality; rudeness; individualistic style of dress. His mother became increasingly unable to cope with him and the school received little effective support. By the fourth form Peter's reports were as follows:

Physics (Target CSE)	Some improvement in effort but still underachieving. By far the most able member of the group.
Maths (Target O level)	Poor attendance, poor attitude, little work, poor level of performance.
English (Target CSE)	Poor level of performance. Finds it difficult to maintain concentration.
Computer Studies (Target O level/ CSE)	Peter has real ability for this subject and at times is way ahead of anyone else in the group in both understanding and use of concepts. However, his attitude to work is so poor that his standard of written work has fallen off dramatically.

Peter subsided into amiable loutishness. He consistently underperformed and his general attitude was one of relaxed sloppiness. He was not averse to making life difficult for his teachers in a quiet way, but never summoned up enough energy to be really difficult. His main medium of protest was his dress which whilst conforming to school colours was a cross between Adam Ant and Dick Whittington. There was never any overt challenge to school authority in later years, just a sad waste of much ability.

Nick

Age on entry	11 years 3 months
VRQ	111
NVRQ	126
Father	Dustman. Parents separated.
Mother	Mother has custody.
Siblings	One older sister.

Primary report
A boy of innate ability – finds settling down extremely difficult ... will have to change considerably. Can be a nuisance – not nastily so – constantly wants to interfere with others. Is very very untidy and easily distracted.

First-year secondary report

English	... poor spelling and poor handwriting ... little knowledge of basic rules ... lacks concentration and is very disorganized ... unwilling to sort himself out.

Maths	... potentially disruptive, needs constant personal supervision ... could do very well.
Science	... poor presentation, little concentration ...

Nick's behaviour in school and outside was a cause for grave concern. He had appeared in court and been found guilty of theft, assault and criminal damage. In school he was inattentive, fidgety, indolent, disorganized, outlandishly dressed in scruffy clothes, and a regular truant.

Throughout his time in school we made no progress with Nick despite strenuous efforts on the part of a number of staff to form a relationship with him. He was controlled by the 'system' but never even looked like beginning to fulfil his potential.

Fourth-year report

English (Target CSE)	... Very capable, very lazy ...
Maths (Target CSE)	... ready understanding, good numerical skills ... unwilling to practise techniques, seldom brings the necessary tools and equipment ... presentation poor ...
Physics (Target CSE)	... able but lazy ...
Computer Studies (Target O level)	... reasonably successful ...

Graham

Age on entry	11 years 5 months
VRQ	108
NVRQ	135
Father	Skilled manual work: engineering.
Mother	Canteen assistant.
Siblings	Eldest son.

Primary report
... artistic and scientific activities very good ... easily led by rougher boys ... gets over excited and noisy ... reads slowly and carefully but is easily distracted.

First-year secondary report

English	... generally satisfactory ... occasionally extremely good ... technically reasonably accurate, mistakes due to carelessness.
Maths	... standard good, although there is room for improvement ...
Science	... an excellent start to his work in science ...

Graham has never presented the school with a 'discipline' problem; our only concern has been his tendency towards being too quiet and withdrawn.

Fourth-year report

English	... still prone to mistakes in language work ... his
(Grades ABA)	literature work is brilliant ...
Maths	... a gifted member of the group ...
(Grades BBB)	
Physics	
(Grades AAA)	
Computer	... shows real command of the subject ....
Studies	
(Grades AAA)	

All these are O level groups. The grades in order refer to effort, level of attainment in the set (all top sets), examination performance. Graham is expected to read for his A levels and then go on to university.

In conclusion
These personal profiles highlight a problem to which there is no simple solution, but a number of strategies can be developed to help such pupils realize their full potential.

1 A senior member of staff is given specific responsibility for:
identifying intelligent under-achievers,
initiating programmes,
spearheading innovation,
monitoring progress.
This member of staff will hold overall responsibility for the school's programme but will work closely with the teacher responsible for in-service education, the Head of Remedial Department, pastoral staff, and so on.
2 The development of staff awareness of the problem and the development of strategies to remedy identified failings. This can be part of the school's programme of in-service education, e.g. visiting speakers at staff meetings, workshop sessions, day conferences, analysis of good practice within the school, group visits to observe work in other schools.
3 The involvement of departments in an analysis and discussion of the problem. Curriculum development and methodological innovation at departmental level should seek to improve the subject provision for all pupils. Departmental staff must be aware of the intellectual potential of pupils and devise schemes of work and methods of learning designed to motivate and challenge all pupils, particularly those of high potential

but little apparent commitment. Imaginative, open-ended work is essential if we are to begin to make headway with our pupils.

4   The development of a rich 'cultural' life in the school. The involvement of pupils in extra-curricular clubs – drama, music, art, chess, creative writing workshops etc. Very able pupils often have many talents and success in a 'non-academic' sphere will often pay rich dividends in a pupil's attitude to normal subjects. (For example, a recalcitrant under-achiever was redeemed at Westlake by being involved in the school play and giving a masterful performance as Macbeth.)

5   A coherent programme of evaluation is essential. The work of all pupils is regularly scrutinized with a view to taking positive action with under-achievers, and departmental programmes of work are constantly examined both internally and by the Governing Body as to their suitability for pupils of all abilities.

6   The development of a school ethos in which pupils can work in the knowledge that all their achievements will be recognized and respected by both their teachers and their peer group. Pupils are also encouraged to think for themselves, to express their own ideas openly, and to be open with staff. This involves a tremendous commitment on the part of teaching staff, many of whom put in many hours above and beyond the call of duty. A great deal of individual counselling, guidance, and support is given, and we have generated an ethos of friendliness within the framework of good discipline.

7   We are consciously seeking to appoint creative, imaginative, committed teachers, who have the ability to get pupils involved in thinking, talking, writing, acting, painting, drawing, making music, and so on, moving away from the concept that intelligence equals the ability to recall facts and to write neatly. This involves the recognition that much learning is an individual process requiring the sophisticated organization of resources and teacher commitment to each pupil.

Having said all this, we recognize that most of what is said applies to all pupils regardless of ability. We believe that whereas school was once perhaps a means to an end, it is now an end in itself. It therefore behoves us to strive to make school a place where every youngster achieves something like his/her full potential and does so in as enjoyable a manner as possible. School should become a place of personal achievement which generates a feeling of self-respect.

The strategies briefly outlined above are not a panacea for all our ills. Indeed we recognize that much has been left unsaid on many subjects such as individualized learning, schemes of self-monitoring, mixed-ability teaching and so on. Nevertheless they are, hopefully, a step along the road towards achieving the goal we have set ourselves.

Reference

[1]The group test scores cited in the following case studies which have been taken from primary school records and are the results of NFER Group Tests of Intelligence CD and DH.

Further Reading

Part One: Identifying very able pupils

ARMSTRONG, H. G. (1967) Wastage of ability among the intellectually gifted *British Journal of Educational Psychology*, 37, 2, 257–9

BARRON, F. (1969) *Creative Person and Creative Process* New York: Holt, Rinehart & Winston

BARBER, W. B. and RENZULLI, J. S. (1975) *Psychology and Education of the Gifted* 2nd edition New York: Irvington

BLOSSER, G. H. (1963) Group intelligence tests as screening devices in locating gifted and superior students in the ninth grade *Exceptional Children*, 29, 6, 282–6

BRANCH, M. and CASH, A. (1966) *Gifted Children* London: Souvenir Press

BRIDGES, S. A. (1973) *IQ 150* Brighton, Sussex: Priory Press

DES (1977) *Gifted Children in Middle and Comprehensive Schools*, London: Longman

EYSENCK, H. J. (1967) 'Intelligence Assessment' *British journal of Educational Psychology* 37 (Feb.), 81–98

GALLAGHER, J. J. (1966) *Research Summary on Gifted Child Education* Dept. of Program Development for Gifted Children, Illinois.

GETZELS, J. W. (1964) 'Creative Thinking, Problem-Solving and Instruction'. *63rd Yearbook Nat. Soc. Stud. Education* Pt 1. 240–67.

GETZELS, J. W. and JACKSON, P. W. (1962) *Creativity and Intelligence: Explorations with Gifted Students* New York: John Wiley

GHISELIN, B. (ed.) (1952) *The Creative Process: A Symposium* California: Univ. California Press

GHISELIN, B. (1963) 'The creative process and its relation to the identification of creative talent' in Taylor, C. W. and Barron, F. (eds.) *Scientific Creativity: Its Recognition and Development* New York: John Wiley

GUILFORD, J. P. (1967) *The Nature of Human Intelligence* New York: McGraw-Hill

HILDRETH, G. H, (1966) *Introduction to the Gifted* New York: McGraw-Hill

HITCHFIELD, E. M. (1973) *In Search of Promise* London: Longman

HOLLINGWORTH, L. S. (1942) *Children above 180 IQ* New York World Book Co.

HOYLE, E. (1969) *Gifted Children and Their Education* London: HMSO

JACOBS, J. C. (1971) Effectiveness of teacher and parent identification of gifted children as a function of school levels *Psychology in the Schools* 8, 2, 140–2

JACOBS, J. C. (1970) Are we being misled by fifty years of research on our gifted children? *Gifted Child Quarterly* 14, Summer, 120–3

KELLMER-PRINGLE, M. L. (1970) *Able Misfits* London: Longman

KERRY, T. (ed.) (1983) *Finding and Helping the Able Child* London: Croom Helm

LYON, H. C. (1976) 'Realizing our potential' in *Gifted Children: Looking to Their Future* London: Latimer

NEWLAND, T. E. (1976) *The Gifted in Socio-Educational Perspective* New Jersey: Prentice Hall

OGILVIE, E. (1970) *Gifted Children in Primary Schools* Schools Council Research Studies London: Harper and Row

PEGNATO, C. W. and BIRCH, J. W. (1959) Locating gifted children in junior high schools: A comparison of methods *Exceptional Children* 25, 7, 300–4.

POVEY, R. (ed.) (1980) *Educating the Gifted Child* London: Harper and Row

RENZULLI, J. (1971) *Scale for the Rating of Behavioural Characteristics of Superior Students* University of Connecticut: Storrs

RENZULLI, J. and SMITH, L. H. (1977) Two approaches to the identification of gifted students *Exceptional Children* 43, pp. 512 *ff.*

ROTH, J. and SUSSMAN, S. (1974) *Educating Gifted Children* York: Ontario Board of Education

SHILEDS, J. B. (1968) *The Gifted Child* Slough: NFER

TEMPEST, N. R. (1974) *Teaching Clever Children 7–11* London: Routledge & Kegan Paul

TERMAN, L. M. *et al. Genetic Studies of Genius* Stanford California: Stanford University Press (Vol. I 1925; Vol. II 1926; Vol. III 1930; Vol. IV 1947; Vol. V 1959.)

TORRANCE, E. P. (1962) *Guiding Creative Talent* New Jersey: Prentice Hall

TUCKMAN, B. W. (1975) *Measuring Educational Outcomes: Fundamentals of Testing* New York: Harcourt, Brace Jovanovich Inc.

VERNON, P. E. (1977) *Gifted Children* London: Methuen

VERNON, P. E., ADAMSON, G. and VERNON, D. F. (1971) *The Psychology and Education of Gifted Children* London: Methuen

WADDINGTON, M. (1961) *Problems of Educating Gifted Young Children with Special Reference to Britain* London: Evans

WALL, W. D. (1960) Highly intelligent children Part 1: The psychology of the gifted; Part 2: The education of the gifted, *Educational Research* 2, 2, 101–10; 2, 3, 207–17

Part Two: Providing for very able pupils

BERNSTEIN, B. (1967) Open schools, open society *New Society* 259, 14 Sept.

BISHOP, W. E. (1968) Successful teachers of the gifted *Exceptional Children* 34, 317–25

BLOOM, B. S. (1973) 'Individual differences in school achievement: a vanishing point?' in Rubin, L. J. *et al.* (1973) *Facts and Feelings in the Classroom* London: Ward Lock Educational

BLOOM, B. S. (1965) *Taxonomy of Educational Objectives* London: Longman

BRUNER, J. S. (1960) *The Process of Education* Harvard: Harvard University Press

BURT, C. L. (1975) *The Gifted Child* London: Hodder & Stoughton

CAVE, R. G. (1971) *An Introduction to Curriculum Development* London: Ward Lock Educational

CRONE, R. and MALONE, J. (1979) *Continuities in Education* Slough: NFER

DES (1977) *Gifted Children in Middle and Comprehensive Schools* London: HMSO

DES (1978) *Primary Education in England* London: HMSO

DES (1978) *Mixed-Ability Work in Comprehensive Schools* London: HMSO

DES (1979) *Aspects of Secondary Education in England* London: HMSO

DEVLIN, T. and WARNOCK, M. (1977) *What Must We Teach?* London: Maurice Temple Smith

DOLL, R. C. (1978) *Curriculum Improvement* Boston: Allyn & Bacon

GALLAGHER, J. J. (1975) *Teaching the Gifted Child* Boston: Allyn & Bacon

GALLAGHER, J. J. (1979) *Reaching Their Potential* Israel: Kolleck & Son

HOLT, M. (1980) *Schools and Curriculum Change* London: McGraw-Hill

HOLT, M. (1979) *The Common Curriculum* London: Routledge & Kegan Paul

HOOPER, R. (ed.) (1973) *The Curriculum* London: Oliver & Boyd

KELLY, A. V. (1977) *The Curriculum* London: Harper & Row

KERRY, T. (1980) The demands made by RE on pupils' thinking *British Journal of Religious Education* 13, 46–52

KINDRED, L. W. *et al.* (1976) *The Middle School Curriculum* London: Allyn & Bacon

KIRK, S. A. and GALLAGHER, J. J. (1979) *Educating Exceptional Children* Boston: Houghton Mifflin

KRAMER, A. H. (1981) *Gifted Children* New York: Trillium Press

KRATHWOHL, D. R. *et al.* (1964) *Taxonomy of Educational Objectives: II Affective Domain* London: Longman

LAWTON, D. *et al.* (1978) *Theory and Practice of Curriculum Studies* London: Routledge & Kegan Paul

MAKER, C. J. (1975) *Training Teachers for the Gifted and Talented: A Comparison of Models* Reston, V.A.: Council for Exceptional Children

NELSON, J. D. and CLELAND, D. L. (1975) 'The role of the teacher of gifted and creative children' in BARBE, WALKER and RENZULLI, J. S. *Psychology and Education of the Gifted* 2nd edition New York: Irvington Publishers

POVEY, R. (ed.) (1980) *Educating the Gifted Child* London: Harper & Row

RATH, J. N. (1971) Teaching without specific objectives *Educ. Leadership* April, 714–20

SANDS, M. K. and KERRY, T. (1982) *Mixed Ability Teaching* London: Croom Helm

SCHOOLS COUNCIL (1972) *With Objectives in Mind: Guide to Science 5–13* London: Macdonald Educational

SCHOOLS COUNCIL (1973) *Pattern and Variation in Curriculum Development Projects: A Study of the Schools Council's Approach to Curriculum Development* London: Macmillan

SCHOOLS COUNCIL (1975) *The Curriculum in the Middle Years* London: Evans/Methuen

SKILLBECK, M. (1971) 'Strategies of curriculum change' in WALTON, J. (ed.) *Curriculum Organization and Design* London: Ward Lock Educational

STENHOUSE, L. (1975) *An Introduction to Curriculum Research and Development* London: Heinemann Educational

TEMPEST, N. R. (1974) *Teaching Clever Children 7–11* London: Routledge & Kegan Paul

TOFFLER, A. (1981) *The Third Wave* London: Penguin

TORRANCE, E. P. (1962) *Guiding Creative Talent* New Jersey: Prentice-Hall

TORRANCE, E. P. (1965) *The Gifted Child in the Classroom* New York: Macmillan

VERNON, P. E. *et al.* (1977) *The Psychology and Education of Gifted Children* London: Methuen

WALTON, J. (1972) *The Secondary School Timetable* London: Ward Lock Educational

WESTON, P. B. (1977) *Framework for the Curriculum* Slough: NFER

WESTON, P. B. (1979) *Negotiating the Curriculum* Slough: NFER

Additional Bibliography

ANASTASI, A. (1961) *Psychological Testing* 2nd edition. New York: Macmillan

BLENKIN, G. M. and KELLY, A. V. (1981) *The Primary Curriculum* London: Harper & Row

BRIDGES, S. A. (1973) *IQ 150* Sussex: Priory Press

BRUNER, J. (1973) *Beyond the Information Given* New York: W. W. Norton

CLARK, B. (1979) *Growing up Gifted: Developing the Potential of Children at Home and at School* Ohio: Charles E. Merrill

DE BONO, E. (1972) *Children Solve Problems* Harmondsworth: Penguin

DEVON EDUCATION COMMITTEE (1977) *Find the Gifted Child* Devon Education Department

FREEMAN, J. (1979) *Gifted Children: Their Identification and Development in a Social Context* Lancaster: MIP Press

FREEMAN, J., BUTCHER, H. J. and CHRISTIE, T. (1971) *Creativity: A Selective View of Research* London: Society for Research into Higher Education

FRENCH, J. (1964) *Educating the Gifted* New York: Holt, Rinehart & Winston

GAGNE, R. M. (ed.) (1967) *Learning and Individual Differences* Ohio: Charles E. Merrill

GEORGE, W. C., SOLANO, C. H. and STANLEY, J. C. *The Gifted and the Creative* Revised and expanded proceedings of the seventh Annual Hyman Blumberg Symposium on Research in Early Childhood Education Baltimore: Johns Hopkins University Press

GEORGE, W. C., COHN, S. J. and STANLEY, J. C. (1979) *Educating the Gifted: Acceleration and Enrichment* Revised and expanded proceedings of the ninth annual Blumberg Symposium on Research in Early Childhood Education Baltimore: Johns Hopkins University Press

GIBSON, J. and CHENNELS, P. (1976) *Gifted Children: Looking to Their Future* Proceedings of the First World Conference on Gifted Children London: National Association for Gifted Children

GOLDSTEIN, S. and FARRAR, D. (1982) *Giftedness: An Annotated Bibliography* School of Education, University of Bath

GRUBB, D. H. W. (ed.) (1982) *The Gifted Child at School* Oxford Society for Applied Studies in Education

HEIM, A. W. (1954) *The Appraisal of Intelligence* London: Methuen

HILDRETH, G. (1964) *Introduction to the Gifted* New York: McGraw-Hill

HITCHFIELD, E. M. (1973) *In Search of Promise: A Long-Term National Study of Able Children and Their Families* London: Longman/National Children's Bureau

HOLLINGWORTH, L. (1942) *Children above 180 IQ* World Book Company

HOPKINSON, D. (1978) *The Education of Gifted Children* London: Woburn Press

HUDSON, L. (1966) *Contrary Imaginations* Harmondsworth: Penguin

JACKSON, B. (1980) *YourExceptional Child* London: Fontana

KOESTLER, A. (1964) *The Act of Creation* London: Hutchinson

LAWTON, D. (1973) *Social Change, Educational Theory and Curriculum Planning* London: Hodder & Stoughton

LAYCOCK, F. (1979) *Gifted Children* Brighton, Sussex: Scotts Foresman

MACINTOSH, H. G. and SMITH, L. (1974) *Towards a Freer Curriculum* London: University of London Press

MUSGRAVE, P. W. (1968) *The School as an Organization* London: Macmillan

NICHOLS, A. and NICHOLS, S. H. (1978) *Developing a Curriculum: A Practical Guide* 2nd edition. London: Allen & Unwin

OGILVIE, E. (1973) *Gifted Children in Primary Schools* Schools Council/Macmillan Education

PRINGLE, M. L. K. (1970) *Able Misfits: A Study of Educational and Behaviour Difficulties of 103 Very Intelligent Children* London: Longman/National Bureau for Cooperation in Child Care

RAPH, J. (1966) *Bright Under-Achievers* New York: Teachers College Press

RAVEN, J. C. (1948) The comparative assessment of intellectual ability *Brit. J. Psychology* 39, 12–19

ROSENTHAL, R. and JACOBSON, L. (1966) Teachers' expectancies: determinants of pupils' IQ gains *Psychol. Reports* 19, 115–18

ROWLANDS, P. (1974) *Gifted Children and Their Problems* London: Dent

RUBIN, L. (1977) *Curriculum Handbook: The Disciplines, Current Movements, Instructional Methodology, Administration and Theory* (abr. ed.) London: Allyn & Bacon

SANDERLIN, O. (1979) *Gifted Children: How to Identify and Teach Them* New Jersey: A. S. Barnes

SCHOOLS COUNCIL (1965) *Curriculum Development: Teachers' Groups and Centres* Working Paper No. 10 London: HMSO

SCHOOLS COUNCIL (1975) *The Whole Curriculum 13–16* Working Paper No. 53 London: Evans/Methuen

SMITH, I. M. (1964) *Spatial Ability: Its Educational and Social Significance* London: University of London Press

STANLEY, J. C., GEORGE, W. C. and SOLANO, C. H. (eds.) *The Gifted and the Creative: A Fifty-Year Perspective* Baltimore: Johns Hopkins University Press

START, A. (1973) *The Gifted Child: A Select Annotated Bibliography* Slough: NFER

STENHOUSE, L. (1968) The humanities curriculum project *Journal of Curriculum Studies* 1, 26–33

STEVENS, A. (1980) *Clever Children in Comprehensive Schools* Harmondsworth: Penguin

TABA, H. (1962) *Curriculum Development: Theory and Practice* New York: Harcourt, Brace & World

TERMAN, L. M. and MERRIL, M. A. (1937) *Measuring Intelligence* London: Harrap

TRUMP, L. J. and MILLER, D. F. (1979) *Secondary School Curriculum Improvement: Meeting Challenges of the Time* London: Allyn & Bacon

VERNON, P. E. (ed.) (1970) *Creativity* Harmondsworth: Penguin

VERNON, P. E. (1977) *The Psychology and Education of Gifted Children* London: Methuen

WECHSLER, D. (1958) *The Measurement and Appraisal of Adult Intelligence* 4th edition London: Ballière, Tindall and Cox

WHEELER, D. K. (1967) *Curriculum Process* London: University of London Press

WHITMORE, J. R. (1980) *Giftedness, Conflict and Under-Achievement* Boston: Allyn & Bacon

WILES, J. and BONDS, J. (1979) *Curriculum Development: A Guide to Practice* Ohio: Charles E. Merrill

WOOD, D. N. (1973) *Teaching Gifted Children* London: Warne

Index